PRAISE FOR THE
ROCK&ROLL
LITERACY SHOW
FROM EDUCATORS AND PARENTS

"I think it would be great to have you speak at a teachers' convention. Your writing message is simple yet so effective. We teachers (and especially the consultants) get caught up in the newest pedagogy sometimes to the detriment of the students."
–SUNNINGDALE ELEMENTARY SCHOOL, MOOSE JAW, SASKATCHEWAN

"The *Rock & Roll Literacy* presentation captivated both the students and teachers. Sigmund gave our teachers and students valuable tips about the writing process, how to get ideas, and he connected it all with high-energy music that motivated and sustained the attention and engagement of the students as he shared."
–CLAXTON ELEMENTARY SCHOOL, KNOXVILLE, TENNESSEE

"Thanks again for the excellent presentation yesterday— everyone was buzzing about it today! Many of the teachers tried the writing activities in the teachers' resource package you sent, and at lunch they were raving about how engaged the kids were. One of our grade three boys even said to his teacher, 'I'm hookin' ya!' Awesome."
–PARK AVENUE PUBLIC SCHOOL, HOLLAND LANDING, ONTARIO

"Thank you so much for taking the time to do the writing workshop. It was a huge success."
–SUCCESS-IN-MIND LEARNING SCHOOL, LEESBURG, VIRGINIA

"My most reluctant reader, who never reads anything but *Spiderman*, *Batman* or *Incredible Hulk* books, has now read most of your books, and has started asking me for the *Narnia* books and the *Lord of the Rings*. Keep motivating students and writing great books."

—WINKLER ELEMENTARY SCHOOL, WINKLER, MANITOBA

"I believe that your comments will have a far-reaching effect. So many valuable life lessons came through. By the way, one of my 'non-readers' just came by my desk to tell me that he is already in chapter six of one of your sports novels. They loved you!"

—GRASSLANDS MIDDLE SCHOOL, FRANKLIN, TENNESSEE

"Just to let everyone know, we had author Sigmund Brouwer at our school this morning! HE WAS ONE OF THE BEST presenters we have ever had. The students and staff were thrilled, entertained and inspired by the presentation."

—WILLOW LANDING ELEMENTARY SCHOOL, BARRIE, ONTARIO

"Several teachers remarked that it was one of the best author presentations they've ever experienced. Bravo!"

—GLANFORD MIDDLE SCHOOL, VICTORIA, BRITISH COLUMBIA

"We all had a blast. One of the fourth-grade teachers told the principal that we should have you every year. Mr. Robison hasn't stopped grinning from ear to ear yet. The kids are browsing your books. It was an unforgettable experience. We are all excited about writing stories."

—KITTRELL ELEMENTARY SCHOOL, MURFREESBORO, TENNESSEE

"I have never seen the kids so hyped-up about a presentation or about writing as they were when they came back [from the *Rock & Roll Literacy* Show]."

—HUMBOLDT COLLEGIATE INSTITUTE, HUMBOLDT, SASKATCHEWAN

"We, as teachers, love the way the excitement continues for such a long time after you leave. I just now had a student say, 'I have never thought of writing that way.' Another student said, 'I liked the way he talked about us becoming better writers instead of just talking about his books.' Keep in touch. We love hearing from you!"

—WORTHINGTON CHRISTIAN SCHOOL, COLUMBUS, OHIO

"[Sigmund Brouwer] did more for literacy in twenty minutes than anyone has in five years…he gets it!"

—STRATHROY DISTRICT COLLEGIATE INSTITUTE, STRATHROY, ONTARIO

"Thanks again for your fabulous presentation here at NCI. I heard lots of rave reviews throughout the day. My students are just itching to grab a pencil and come up with crazy story lines."

—NIVERVILLE COLLEGIATE INSTITUTE SCHOOL, NIVERVILLE, MANITOBA

"I just wanted to thank you so much for coming to our school last week. The students are still talking about your visit and asking for your books. We asked students from all grades what they really thought of your visit. The responses were amazing. The elementary teachers have already had the students begin writing using the three points you told them. They are very pleased with the results."

—BEARSPAW SCHOOL, CALGARY, ALBERTA

ROCK & ROLL LITERACY

SIGMUND BROUWER

ORCA BOOK PUBLISHERS

Library and Archives Canada Cataloguing in Publication

Brouwer, Sigmund, 1959-
Rock & roll literacy / written by Sigmund Brouwer.

Issued also in an electronic format.
ISBN 978-1-55469-358-0

1. Reading. 2. Creative writing--Study and teaching. 3. Literacy--
Study and teaching. I. Title. II. Title: Rock and roll literacy.
LB1050.B76 2011   428.4   C2011-903330-5

First published in the United States, 2011
Library of Congress Control Number: 2011929248

Summary: Sigmund Brouwer brings his unique sense of play
to the serious business of learning to read and write.

MIX
Paper from
responsible sources
FSC® C016245

FSC
www.fsc.org

*Orca Book Publishers is dedicated to preserving the environment and has printed this book
on paper certified by the Forest Stewardship Council®.*

Orca Book Publishers gratefully acknowledges the support for its publishing programs provided by the
following agencies: the Government of Canada through the Canada Book Fund and
the Canada Council for the Arts,
and the Province of British Columbia through the BC Arts Council and the Book Publishing Tax Credit.

Cover design by Teresa Bubela
Cover photography by Reba Baskett

ORCA BOOK PUBLISHERS   ORCA BOOK PUBLISHERS
PO Box 5626, Stn. B   PO Box 468
Victoria, BC Canada   Custer, WA USA
v8R 6s4   98240-0468

www.rockandroll-literacy.com
www.orcabook.com
Printed and bound in Canada.

14 13 12 11 • 4 3 2 1

CL
428.4
crl

9/11

To Andrew, Bob, Sarah and everyone else at Orca—from the front desk to the warehouse and everywhere in between. Thanks for the amazing boost you've given to Rock & Roll Literacy.

And to Doc Ivan—thanks for great conversations, compelling arguments and, most of all, for helping my little girl's smile become even more beautiful.

CONTENTS

INTRODUCTION xi

PART ONE—UNDERSTAND STORY 1

1. The Princess Bride 2
2. Story Is Everything 8
3. Make the Connection 12
4. Know Your Audience 17

PART TWO—TEACH STORY 23

5. A Very Large Orchestra 24
6. Doc Ivan 28
7. A Little Boy Attached to Every Story 31
8. Twenty Percent Mechanics 37
9. Assembly Line 42
10. When Information Matters Most 49
11. The Gender Difference 55

PART THREE—WRITE STORY 61

12. Motivation 62
13. Daydreams and Research 66
14. Story Structure 71
15. Seriously, What Is Story Structure? 72
16. Story's Engine 73
17. Hide the Thumb 76

PART FOUR—REVISE STORY 79

18. Never Write Beyond the Headlights 80
19. Writing Is Difficult 86
20. Teaching Revision 89
21. The Writing Pyramid 95
22. Pyramid Base: Revising Story 97
23. Pyramid Middle: Word Choice 101
24. Pyramid Middle: Adjectives and Adverbs 105
25. Pyramid Middle: Redundancy 108
26. Pyramid Middle: Five Senses 111
27. Pyramid Middle: Word Count 113
28. Pyramid Tip: Spelling 115
29. Pyramid Tip: Grammar 118
30. Pyramid Tip: Punctuation............................ 122
31. Joey's Run Away Horse 123

SOME FINAL THOUGHTS 127

INTRODUCTION

Thanks for letting me share *Rock & Roll Literacy* with you.

I take this privilege very seriously, mainly because of an unexpected phone call from a stranger. The call came a couple of years after I began presenting at schools. Until then, my school appearances had been all about fun—for me and for the students.

The woman on the phone that night started crying after I confirmed that I was indeed the author who had been at a certain school; I braced myself to hear what I'd done to upset her.

She blurted out that her son, who was in grade four, hated reading but had made it through one of my sports novels and asked for the next one. She wanted to thank me for getting him interested in reading. She apologized for her tears, but said she couldn't help crying, because it meant so much to her.

I'd like to take the credit for that gratitude, but I'm not sure any visiting author ever deserves it.

Her thanks should have gone to the teachers who never gave up on her son. He was only able to read my book because, from kindergarten on, teachers had patiently introduced him to the strange shapes of the alphabet, and then to the way words sound. They taught him how to read, not me.

Teachers till the soil and plant the seed; teachers add water and keep nurturing. I just happened along at the right time, adding a little more sunlight. The seedling that had been slowly growing beneath the surface of the soil finally broke through.

I love the chance to do my part, and since that phone call, my biggest motivation in any *Rock & Roll Literacy* show has been to reach at least one non-reading rascal somewhere in the gym, a rascal whose teacher has already taken him most of the way.

This non-reading rascal is often a boy, and I use "guy" stories to try to connect.

If I ever have a chance to visit you and your students—and I hope I do—I'm very careful to balance my silly stories with more serious material, which keeps the good readers engaged, including the girls in the audience. I'll stress, for example, that *Anne of Green Gables* is probably the best example of story— ever. Even if you're a guy!

What I'm trying to do in my presentations is give students a sense of purpose as they write. For all your students at all levels, my foundational writing advice—either during a presentation or in this book—is meant to mesh with the techniques you teach in the classroom.

I'd appreciate your input, and I'll share your advice with other teachers on my website, rockandroll-literacy.com. I'll do my best to learn from your advice. You can send comments, as well as questions about booking my presentation, to rockandroll-literacy.com.

Again, thanks for the chance to be part of your teaching journey.

Sigmund Brouwer

AT THE EARLY STAGES of writing this book, my editor, Sarah, smiled and said, "Sigmund, my sense about all of this is that you see yourself as a champion for all those little guys who hate reading and writing."

She's right. This is one area where—sorry for the cliché—my heart is on my sleeve. No matter how many published books I might be able to hold up as I speak to a gymful of kids, inside I'm still the twelve-year-old boy who was told by his teacher, in front of all his classmates, that his writing was stupid. (See Chapter 7.)

I feel for all the kids out there who struggle with writing, and I think there are things about the curriculum system of teaching writing that hurt them. Especially after that phone call from the crying mother, I always try to reach those same kids with a message of encouragement.

PART 1

UNDERSTAND STORY

CHAPTER 1

THE PRINCESS BRIDE

At 8:45 on a cold winter morning at a school in Saskatchewan, I had finished sound-checking my gear. With less than five minutes until the students were due to arrive, the librarian paced tight circles nearby, the sound of her high heels clicking in the empty gym.

"Are you nervous?" I asked.

"No," she said. Pause. "Okay. Yes."

"About the presentation?"

If so, I understood. It's always a risk when a principal or a librarian brings in a speaker. If the speaker does a bad job or offends the audience, the blame falls on the person who invited the speaker.

"Anything in the content of my presentation you would like me to change?" I said. Public speaking is a tightrope act. Totally safe is totally boring. It takes provocation of sorts to hold an audience's interest. I want to help teachers motivate their reluctant readers and writers. That means I will occasionally—okay, nearly always—talk about boogers and other gross stuff, like firing a poopy diaper from a giant slingshot. I run the outline of my presentation past the librarian and principal ahead of time so there are no surprises. I'm mortified at the possibility of offending any teachers or parents.

"It's not that," she said. Hesitation. "In the staff room this morning, some of the teachers wondered if this was a smart thing to do. Get everybody in the gym for an hour. To listen to an author."

Everybody meant grades one through eight. It was a lower-income school, she explained, with lots of discipline problems.

Four minutes remained until the first students would arrive. The first of four hundred students. The gym would be packed.

"They think I'm in trouble," I said.

"They think," she continued, "it's going to be like throwing a pork chop in front of wolves. They say we should have done this in small groups instead. You know, so they'll listen. These kids can get out of control."

Four hundred kids, ranging in age from six to fourteen, sitting on the cold floor of the gym. Mine for an hour.

"Don't worry about me," I said.

"No?"

"No," I said. "If it's a disaster, I'll be gone and everyone will blame you."

She moaned. My comment was funny to me, I guess, but not so much to her. (That happens to me. A lot.)

We heard chatter from the hallway. The kids were arriving early. The first of them stepped into the gym. The grade eights. Some of them wearing ball caps turned backward. None of them smiling.

"It will be okay," I told her.

I knew something she didn't know.

There wasn't enough time to tell her about the best sword-fighting scene ever in cinematic history. If you've seen *The Princess Bride* you know the scene. Westley, on his way to rescue the love of his life, finds Inigo Montoya at the top of the Cliffs of Insanity, sword in hand, with orders to kill Westley.

It's a gentlemanly fight—lots of sword-clashing and conversation throughout. Both Westley and Montoya begin their duel left-handed.

Because Montoya has trained for years and is one of the best left-handed swordsmen alive, he's a little puzzled that an unknown sword fighter like Westley manages to defend himself so well. But Montoya is cheerful, and finally Westley asks him why.

"I know something you don't know," Montoya answers. "I am not left-handed."

With that Montoya throws his sword from his left hand to his right hand, and presses forward, coming precariously close to defeating Westley.

But Westley remains equally cheerful, until Montoya, still puzzled, comments on Westley's good humor.

Westley's answer, as he throws his sword to his right hand: "I know something you don't know. I am not left-handed either."

When facing four hundred kids in a gym, I often feel like Westley. There is stress involved. If I don't hold the kids' attention, it *will* be a disaster. In a way, it is like a sword duel; coasting on past success is not an option.

Yet it is positive stress. As the gym continued to fill, with the librarian's nervousness increasing, I wasn't afraid. There's a fine line between cockiness and confidence. I hope you don't sense cockiness as I explain, again like Westley, that I knew something the librarian did not know.

I have become adept, not with a sword—although that would be cool—but with something far more powerful.

Story.

My confidence was not based on believing *my* stories are wonderful. Not at all. It was confidence based on knowing that I was free to use other people's great stories. All of us have that power. It's simply a matter of listening for those stories and retelling them.

Most of the time, I begin my presentations as Montoya did, keeping my right-handed ability in reserve, watching for the moment when the students become restless.

My left-hand story—the one I start with—is about the afternoon I opened a book, expecting to hate it because I was pretty sure there was no action in it. Instead, I was drawn in because of the way the words made pictures in my head. I saw a little girl sitting all alone at a train station, waiting and waiting. Everything she owns is in a shabby, old-fashioned carpet bag. She's an orphan, about to discover that her dream of belonging to a family is not going to come true. There's been a mistake. The family she thinks is going to adopt her wants a boy, not a girl. Mr. Matthew Cuthbert is about to crush her dreams and send her back to the orphanage.

While it no longer surprises me, it never fails to amaze me how silent it is, even with three or four hundred middle-schoolers in a gym, as I describe the beginning of *Anne of Green Gables*. It's not a weird story, a gross story, a violent story, a fast-paced story. It's simply a great story. And just about anywhere, it's enough to hold the students rapt.

On that cold morning in Saskatchewan, though, as the students walked into the gym, I sensed that the librarian's fears were well-founded. Not much eye contact. Lots of attitude.

Even with the rock music playing, none of them seemed engaged. Instead, they looked at me with suspicion.

I knew I wouldn't have Montoya's luxury of easing into this left-handed. *Anne of Green Gables* wouldn't work for these kids. Sometimes, great as *Anne of Green Gables* is, you need a little more.

The last of the students took their places. I cut the music. The librarian introduced me.

"Hi," I said.

No response. Yup, definitely time to put my imaginary sword in my right hand.

"My best friend used to play in the NHL for the Edmonton Oilers," I said. "Guy by the name of Mike Moller. You can see his sweater in the Hockey Hall of Fame. He was on one of the Oiler's Stanley Cup teams."

I paused. A few heads came up—the guys in the back, the oldest guys, who had been staring at the floor. I was in the heart of the Canadian prairies. I could guess their thoughts. *NHL? National Hockey League? You have a friend who played in the NHL? Someone in the Hall of Fame? Someone who won a Stanley Cup?*

"In fact," I continued, after letting that sink in, "he's retired now, but Mike and I play on the same hockey team every Thursday."

I played some college hockey, but at no point was I good enough to get any attention from any scouts. I had no idea that my futile hockey dreams would reward me later, when I was facing kids like these.

You can see, of course, how deliberate—even manipulative—it was to begin my presentation like that, trying to earn some secondhand respect before making a connection with the kids. And I knew something the librarian didn't know.

In my right hand was a story that never fails to interest even the most reluctant readers and writers.

"One night after one of our hockey games," I said, "I asked Mike to tell me about the weirdest thing he'd ever seen in nine years of pro hockey."

I paused. To build expectations, to gauge their interest.

It was there.

"And without even stopping to think about it," I continued, "Mike told me that at the beginning of practice, a guy started stripping in front of the entire team. The guy had just been traded, and Mike said nobody even knew who he was. And with no warning, the guy just stopped skating and started stripping."

No surprise. I had everyone's attention now. Especially the teachers.

Story can do that.

So can stripping.

CHAPTER 2
STORY IS EVERYTHING

As I started to tell the story to that gymful of kids, I remembered Mike's big grin when he first told our hockey team the stripping story. It was after one of our Thursday-night hockey games. We were at a pizza place, enjoying pitchers of, um, ice-cold lemonade.

"Oh yeah," Mike told us as the pizza arrived. "A guy started stripping on the ice. New guy. Just got traded to the team. Early morning practice, steps on the ice late, takes maybe three strides, hits the brakes, fires his gloves and stick as hard as he could across the ice."

You can bet all of us leaned forward to listen to the rest of the story. No surprise, so did the kids in the gym, even the ones with their arms crossed.

Mike described how the guy ripped off his helmet strap, popped his helmet onto the ice, tore off his jersey, yanked off his suspenders and rammed his hockey pants to his ankles. All in silence. The rest of the team on the ice watched, dumbstruck.

The new guy ripped his socks down, grabbed his shin pad and fired it all the way across the ice.

"When it landed," Mike said, his grin even bigger because he knew he had all of us hooked, "cockroaches exploded from the inside of the shin pad. Everywhere. Probably thirty of them, shooting in all directions on the ice. We look back at the new guy; he's firing his other shin pad down the ice. Same thing. Cockroaches everywhere. And he starts brushing them off his chest and belly, scattering bugs along the ice at his feet. Turns out, the night before, he'd hung his equipment in a corner of the dressing room that no one had used all season. There were a bunch of bugs behind the wall. During the night they'd crawled into his equipment, and because he'd dressed in a hurry, he hadn't noticed the bugs. When he started skating, the cockroaches began to move around."

I told the kids in the gym that after hearing Mike's story, I decided immediately to use it as the opening chapter of *Rebel Glory*, one of my hockey novels. I changed a few of the details, but I kept the part of Mike's story where he described the professional athletes on his team skating around like little boys, smashing cockroaches and splattering the bug guts as if they were popping cherry tomatoes.

Halfway through my go-to story that winter morning, all the reluctant readers and writers in the gym leaned forward and began to uncross their arms. They even started to smile. By the time they heard the part about the cockroaches, and about the players smashing the cockroaches, they were fully engaged. Partly because they'd be the first ones to splatter cockroaches too, and partly because so many of the teachers were shaking and grimacing as if there were cockroaches in the gym.

After that, armed with rock and roll music to play during stand-and-stretch breaks, I moved on to a story about a guy getting a wedgie in the penalty box...

Story is everything.

I don't mean plot. I mean the entire package: plot, setting, character, motivation, dialogue, theme. Fiction or nonfiction.

I mean story as in STORY.

We are human because we tell stories. Telling stories makes us human.

Story is the most powerful and effective way to engage and influence people, to shape cultures. More effective and more powerful, in the long term, than either war or diplomacy.

Jokes are stories. Songs are stories. Movies are stories. So is TV. Great paintings are stories. Gossip is stories.

Our collective history is an unfolding story.

Our individual lives are unfolding stories; we share our lives when we share our stories.

We share stories because we are biologically wired to respond to story. We learn from story.

The media uses story to draw us, to spellbind us, to horrify us, to make us cheer or jeer, to make us take action.

Story is everything.

Those who tell us stories hold our attention; those who simply deliver information, often lose our attention. Unless they deliver the information through story.

Story is everything.

I believe we all know this on an unconscious level.

To accept this on a conscious level will give you the power of the Pied Piper (a reference that you understand, of course, through story) to enchant your students.

After all, when you teach—whether in the school system or at home—you are facing an audience, large or small. Among all the motivations we have for teaching, I think the most addictive is the spontaneous and apparently mysterious chemistry that occurs when you make a connection with your audience.

Story is not the only way to make this connection, but it's one of the easiest and most immediate, and it will rarely fail. And while the chemistry of this connection may appear spontaneous, anyone can learn to orchestrate it at will; it doesn't require a "natural" gift.

All you need to understand is where and how story gets its power.

CHAPTER 3

MAKE THE CONNECTION

One of my hockey novels, *Thunderbird Spirit*, begins with a player sitting in the penalty box, halfway through a hockey game. That chapter is a retelling of something that happened to my friend, Peter Anholt, who also played in our Thursday-night hockey games.

Pete played some university and junior hockey and also coached at a high level. Sitting in the dressing room with the team one night before a game, I asked him to tell me about the angriest he had ever been in his hockey career.

"Saskatoon," he said.

The guys in the dressing room stopped lacing their skates. The stick-taping stopped, the quiet conversations stopped.

All it had taken was one word.

Saskatoon.

We knew a story was coming, and all of us were hooked by curiosity.

Pete delivered. "I'm in the penalty box," he said. "We're in town to play the Blades. Third period and a fan is yelling at me."

We waited.

"I ignore the guy, even though he's leaning over the Plexiglas, screaming in my ear. Because the last thing I want is to let him know he's getting to me. It was fun, driving him crazy by ignoring him, until he got so mad he leaned even closer and spit in my face."

"At that point," Pete said, "I lost it. Grabbed the guy by both shoulders."

Now, if we freeze that moment—the two of them, eyes barely inches apart—it underscores my point. Pete and the angry fan were emotionally connected, in a private world of two. Pete's surge of anger consumed him, and it had his hundred-percent focus. He was lost in feelings. No way was Pete distracted by thoughts of what he would eat after the game, or what the consequences might be of what he was about to do.

When we're scared, all we can think about is our fear and how to make it go away. When we're laughing, we are in the moment. Feelings hook us. Completely. We get lost in that feeling.

When I retell Pete's story to a gymful of kids, they, too, think about nothing else except Pete face-to-face with an angry fan. They, too, are hooked by the feelings generated by this story.

It's very, very fun retelling this story, because not one kid is wiggling, not one kid is looking anywhere else except the front of the gym, where I'm acting out what happened after that.

Pete said that when he pulled the guy into the penalty box to fight him, he miscalculated. He yanked so hard, the guy flopped across his lap. Now Pete's looking down, and all he can see is the man's feet, legs, buttocks, back and shoulders.

I'll never forget Pete describing that moment. "What was I going to do next?" he said. "Spank the guy?"

Curiosity, anticipation. Great emotions to hook an audience.

I wish you could have been there, in the dressing room to see Pete's little smile as he continued. "And then I saw the top of the guy's underwear."

Yup. Pete gave the fan a wedgie right to his shoulder blades. Pulled the top of the underwear so high, he said, it was like the guy was wearing a thong. We howled.

Right then, I knew I had a story with great power. And the kids in the gym know it too.

If I can't convince you of the truth of the following sentence, there's no point in you reading the rest of this book: Although we are set apart from the rest of Earth's species by our intellect, we are creatures primarily driven by emotion.

We are not like Spock—half-human hybrids with Vulcan fathers. Glorious and amazing as the human intellect is, far too often we make our decisions based on emotion. Our choices—often irrational—are motivated by greed, fear, love, anger, laziness, hatred.

Example?

Retirement funding. We know we should be saving, but few of us do. If you put a thousand dollars aside today, in thirty years of annual compound interest at 5 percent, it will be worth over $40,000.

So, logically, all of us should be putting aside as much money as possible. Logically, the money that I've spent to acquire every new model of the iPhone should have been put into my retirement funds.

But our hearts tell us something entirely different. Emotion nearly always wins over intellect. We listen to our hearts and spend those dollars on fancy new gadgets or vacations or chocolate desserts.

Television advertising: emotional connection.

Choosing the bad boy over the nice but boring boy: emotional connection.

Giving your full attention to a speaker because he starts by describing someone stripping on the ice: emotional connection.

Winning an argument based strictly on facts—good luck. Winning an argument is usually determined by something else: emotional connection.

The power of story to make an emotional connection is the compelling reason that great convention speakers and pastors and politicians always start their speeches with a story. If all the story did was make a valid intellectual point—and yes, of course, stories are ways to teach—the audience's emotional reaction to the story would not matter.

But emotional reaction *does* matter. A convention speaker or politician is usually a complete stranger to the members of his or her audience, so it is crucial to form an immediate and positive emotional connection with them. Story is the bridge between speaker and audience.

At that presentation in Saskatchewan, I could have opened by trying to appeal to students on an intellectual level, by stressing the importance of reading and writing skills to their future success. That would have gotten me about as far as trying to get them to start saving for their retirements.

Instead, the cockroach story established an immediate emotional connection, and all I needed to do during the remainder of the presentation was use a new story for each new point I wanted to make about the importance of reading and writing in their lives.

While I hope that during a *Rock & Roll Literacy* presentation I appear to be a gifted speaker, the truth is, I am simply taking advantage of the power of story. There is nothing complex about where story gets its power. **A good story, like a good song, makes you feel something.**

Set aside for now all the academic stuff: the symbolism, characterization, writing mechanics, the curriculum connections. These are all just pieces that need to work together to produce a singular result.

Name an emotion. A good story will use that emotion to make the audience curious, keep it in suspense, make it laugh or gross it out.

At the risk of repeating myself, it really is this simple: If a story—or song or any other form of art—doesn't produce or provoke an emotional reaction, it's not working. There is a big difference between recognizing a good story (simple) and creating a good story (not so simple, but still not as complex as you are sometimes led to believe). That's part three of this book.

Which leads to THE most important component of the power of story.

Audience.

CHAPTER 4
KNOW YOUR AUDIENCE

With a bounty hunter and hounds in pursuit, a father hands his daughter a letter he has written her, just before abandoning her and leading the dogs away from her:

Caitlyn,

We had agreed—the woman I loved and I—that as soon as you were born, we would perform an act of mercy and decency and wrap you in a towel to drown you in a nearby sink of water, like a kitten in a sack dropped into a river.

But in the motel room that was our home, the woman I loved died while giving birth. You were a tiny bundle of silent and alert vulnerability and all that remained to remind me of the woman.

I was nearly blind with tears in that lonely motel room. With the selfishness typical of my entire life to that point, I delayed the mercy and decency we had promised you.

I used the towel not to wrap and drown you, but to clean and dry you.

As I lifted your twisted hands and gently wiped the terrible hunch in the center of your back—where your arms connected to a ridge of bone that pushed against your translucent skin—I heard God speak to me for the first time in my life.

God did not speak in the loud and terrible way as claimed by the preachers of Appalachia, where I fled with you. Instead God spoke in the way I believe God most often speaks to humans—through the heart, when circumstances have stripped away our obstinate self-focus.

Holding you in your first moments outside the womb, I was overwhelmed by protective love. Even in the circumstances you face now, believe that my love has only strengthened since then.

I do not regret the price I paid for my love for you. But I do regret what it has cost you, all your life. And I have never stopped regretting all that I kept hidden from you.

This letter comes at the beginning of one of my adult novels, *Broken Angel.*

It led to a contract to write *Broken Angel,* as well as its sequel, *Flight of Shadows.* I didn't submit the completed novel—only the first chapter and a synopsis of the story. My editor for both projects said this letter alone grabbed the publishing committee, and this letter alone led to that two-book contract. She told me the letter had such power that they wanted to read the rest of the novel.

I don't read this piece of writing when I'm presenting to kids in grades K to six. Too intense. But when I read it out loud to middle-school students, the gym gets very, very quiet, matching the tone of that piece of writing. This silence is a very different emotional reaction than I get to the cockroach story, but it is still an emotional reaction.

I hope I've made a convincing argument for story's power to make an emotional connection. If so, it may sound extremely obvious that you first need to understand your audience before deciding what kind of story will hold them.

And yet.

I've led dozens upon dozens of writing seminars for kids of all ages. At every seminar or workshop, I ask someone to tell me the single most important question they need to ask (and answer) before starting a writing project, before committing a single word to paper, indeed before researching, daydreaming the story, or doing any other aspect of writing.

I love the answers I get from the kids, because it gives me immediate insight into what they believe are their writing priorities.

What's the title?

How long should it be?

Do I use pencil or pen?

What's it about?

I find it significant (and somehow endearing) that I have yet to hear this question: *Who am I writing for?*

Most of these students have been taught writing for years. Punctuation and grammar have been drilled into them. They can label parts of sentences and define a topic sentence. But from my perspective, all of these tools will fail them if they don't understand the first and most fundamental aspect of writing: *Who am I writing for?*

If you are hoping to amuse or engage your readers with a story, you'd better know that a story about poopy pants shot from a giant slingshot will go over much better with boys than with most middle-aged women.

If you are writing an instruction manual, you'd better match the complexity with the comprehension level of your reader.

Email? Are you sending it to a close friend or prospective employer? Ask around. Anybody who has been in a hiring position will tell you about kids fresh out of high school who don't understand that there is a difference.

Even if it's obvious to you, I think you need to take great pains to make sure your students understand this first and foremost.

Teachers who put their audience ahead of their message are successful teachers. They examine their lesson plans through their students' eyes, and ask themselves how best to present so that the students understand the material.

During a *Rock & Roll Literacy* show, I don't tell the students to carefully consider the emotional needs of their audience and find a way to connect.

No way. The kids in the gym are a different audience than the readers of this book.

I tell them that when they write a story, their job is to mess with their teachers. Push the teachers' buttons. I want to present this principle in a way that the audience wants to hear.

Naturally, by the time I've told the cockroach story, the wedgie story, the poopy diaper story (I'll get to that), along with a couple of references to boogers, the students—and teachers, my other audience in the gym—have forgotten my earlier insistence that *Anne of Green Gables* is the best book EVER.

That's when I need to bring the students back to the most important thing about story and the writing of stories. Telling stories is not just about the silly stuff.

Always remember: *R-R-R*.

The Right story at the Right time for the Right audience.

Deep Purple's "Smoke on the Water" is a great song to rock the dressing room when the coach wants to pump up the players for a big game. It's not great background music during a romantic dinner. *R-R-R*.

This is what I tell the kids: One week, yes, put stories on paper that make your friends giggle. But the next week, when your teacher asks you to write a story for your grandmother, you'll need to try to push different emotional buttons with stories that aren't about gross stuff.

Once in a while, though, a kid might holler, "My grandmother has silent gas! So she should love a story about it!"

SINCE STORY IS SUCH a powerful way to connect with students, I'd like to suggest a practical use for it in your classroom. Each day, take the first few minutes of class to tell a story that's relevant to that day's curriculum. The emotional connection of a good story will spill over for the rest of the class period. Once students realize you are going to make a habit of telling a story every day, they'll look forward to it.

This works for every curriculum. In math or science, for example, before discussing the mathematical formulas that Newton used to describe motion and gravity, tell your students about the scientist a generation earlier who made it all possible with meticulous observations of the night sky—a man who owned a pet moose, lost his nose during a sword fight and died because he had to pee so bad his bladder burst. Give your students all the juicy details, right down to Tycho Brahe's final words as he succumbed to an infection: "Let me not seem to have lived in vain."

A bit weird and gross?

Sure. But you can bet the students will love it.

Dramatic?

Of course. But fun for you and fun for the class. And very relevant.

PART 2

TEACH STORY

CHAPTER 5
A VERY LARGE ORCHESTRA

I do my best to make my *Rock & Roll Literacy* presentations enjoyable for teachers, but I'm in the gym primarily for reluctant readers and writers, who are easy to spot. Arms crossed, sour expressions on their faces. I'm there to talk about reading and writing, and they don't want anything to do with it.

I'm glad I have some great stories to tell them.

Them.

It's a grind to get this type of student to read and next to impossible to get them to write. We—his teachers, his parents and I—all know this skill is vital to his future success. But that boy in the back row, shooting spitballs whenever you're not looking, grudgingly puts as little as possible onto paper and then hands it in, not caring what grade he gets.

Much as he frustrates us, he also deserves a degree of sympathy. In *The Myth of Laziness*, Dr. Mel Levine argues that many kids with learning disabilities are wrongly labeled as lazy. Levine shows that most students do want to be productive, but give up when they don't feel equipped for the task.

Although *The Myth of Laziness* is not a book about literacy—but very well worth reading and applying to reading and writing—Dr. Levine states that "writing is the largest orchestra a kid's mind has to conduct."

I agree with Dr. Levine when he says, "There's no other requirement that demands the coordination and integration of so many different neurodevelopmental functions and academic subskills."

I certainly agree with his summation of what writing demands of a child: the organization of good ideas, encoded into clear language; juggling the complexity of spelling and punctuation and grammar rules; using the physical coordination of fingers for writing or keyboarding, all framed within time-management skills.

Most of us would agree emphatically with Dr. Levine about the writing process, but unfortunately that same agreement leads us into a trap, because it tempts us to view writing as primarily an intellectual process of mastering specific writing mechanics.

This view results in the reams of sometimes conflicting pedagogical discourse on writing; reams of diverse and changing-with-fashion curriculum material; and reams of intellectual approaches to assessing and grading student writing, much of it focused on the mechanics.

Please understand that I am not critical of learning and sharing these mechanics. Understanding the mechanics is as necessary to the teaching of writing as understanding hockey drills, breakout patterns and power-play analysis is to great hockey coaching.

But hockey is more than just players and coaches mastering the mechanics. NHL Hall of Famer Bryan Trottier, with six Stanley Cups as a player and another Stanley Cup as an assistant coach, will tell you what makes the mechanics function on a winning team: heart.

Great coaches not only thoroughly understand the game, they also have the pulse of the individual players and the pulse of the team. Great coaches know when to encourage their players, when the players need to be left alone, and when it's time to pull a player aside and give him a good kick in the butt. Great coaches understand the chemistry of teamwork, and that sometimes a player with bad attitude can become toxic for the team.

Most importantly, great coaches know that mechanics are simply preparation for something mysterious and difficult to define—the ability of the human spirit to overcome challenge and adversity.

In the same way, the process of writing is much, much more than all the mechanical pieces we try to teach to kids. Writing, because it essentially bares your soul on paper, is the definition of heart.

The trap snaps shut on us when we, as teachers of literacy, focus primarily on the mechanics of writing and forget or ignore the emotional aspects of the process. Then we risk becoming as ineffective as coaches who think all it takes to win games is to understand and apply the mechanics.

Emotion is a crucial factor in learning to read and write.

You can argue that there is no heart or emotion involved in writing or reading an instruction manual or an informational email. I not only agree, I'll go one step further and suggest that, ultimately, our purpose is to prepare our kids to excel at information writing as adults. Few of them will become journalists or novelists or playwrights or poets. All of them are going to need to be able to write clear and concise sentences, whether it is for an email or a business report. Yet writing ability is only gained through the practice of putting words on paper. If our ultimate goal is to prepare kids to write well as adults, we need to understand that what motivates them now happens on an emotional level.

I'm not merely suggesting that the emotional component must be included somewhere along the way. Instead, without diminishing the need to understand and teach mechanics, I believe that the magical, wonderful, dust-on-butterfly-wings process of bringing words to life on paper—for teachers and students—is driven primarily by emotion. I cannot stress this enough—when you are dealing with story, emotion takes precedence over intellect.

After all, we are not teaching robots, we are teaching boys and girls.

CHAPTER 6
DOC IVAN

Life lessons come in all shapes and sizes. Ponytail and braces—that was our ten-year-old daughter Olivia, waiting for Doc Ivan to examine her teeth, a few months into the course of orthodontic treatment.

Olivia wasn't alone at this appointment. It was a family event. My wife Cindy, our younger daughter, Savannah, and I were also in the small room, where images of Olivia's jaw and teeth were displayed on a computer screen.

From what I understand, most orthodontists don't allow the entire family to be part of the consult.

Most orthodontists choose a different layout to maximize space and time efficiency: an open area, with parents waiting seperately while the doctor moves from patient to patient. After an assessment, the orthodontist gives instructions to the child, and also to a dental assistant, who does the necessary mechanical adjustments while the orthodontist moves to the next patient. Moving quickly, an orthodontist can dispense this specialized knowledge to nearly 120 patients per day.

Because I knew how precious time was in a situation like that, and that there were other families in other rooms waiting for Doc Ivan, my stress level rose when he walked into the room and asked Olivia if she had done anything fun on the weekend.

Olivia can talk. And talk. And talk. She loves telling stories. We'd recently gone on a family rafting trip, and she wanted to tell Doc Ivan all about it.

On cue, at every pause in Olivia's story, Doc Ivan clucked with concern, or oohed in admiration, depending on what was appropriate.

My internal response was much different than his external reaction. I wanted the story to be over. Didn't Olivia realize how many other people needed Doc Ivan's time? I waited and waited and waited, my stress level climbing, until her story ended. The only reason I didn't interrupt was because this was Doc Ivan's office; it wasn't my business to tell Doc Ivan how to do his job.

When her story finally did end, he gave her a high five and then checked her braces. Thirty seconds later, he pronounced it was time to put in a more high-tensile wire. He gave Olivia some instructions and asked if she, or my wife or I, had any questions about what Olivia needed to do on a nightly basis. Satisfied that we all knew what was needed, he left with a cheerful goodbye—but not without first giving Savannah his full attention for about a minute so that she wouldn't feel left out. His assistant spent another five minutes explaining the mechanical aspects of complying with his instructions.

Later, in a social situation, I had a chance to ask Doc Ivan about the way he treated his patients. His assessment and instructions took up a very small portion of his time with our family, and to me, it didn't seem efficient—about 80 percent of the consult had been spent on talking to Olivia and Savannah.

Remember I said this was unusual?

In contrast to the orthodontist who efficiently isolates patients in cubicles, Doc Ivan at best can see only 90 patients per day, 30 less than many of his colleagues. From a cold revenue point of view, that's a substantial difference.

Which brings me to the reason for telling this story.

It's very simple.

When I asked Doc Ivan why he runs his practice so differently from other orthodontists, why he would spend five minutes listening to Olivia's story like it was the most important thing he could do at the time, this was his answer: "Sigmund, there's a little girl attached to those teeth."

CHAPTER 7

A LITTLE BOY ATTACHED TO EVERY STORY

I was in the seventh grade when I wrote my first official story for an official grade. I'd written lots of stories at home for fun, but never at school. I was excited about the chance to write a story. Any story. On any subject. A made-up story. A story someone else would read.

Finally, fun writing. This was before computers. (Long before computers.) For me, writing at school to that point had mainly been:

- handwriting exercises (my skill level: horrible)
- putting marks where the syllable needed to be emphasized in a word (no comprehension on this. None.)
- spelling, grammar and punctuation exercises (ability to label gerunds, etc: zero)
- research, and regurgitation of said research, commonly known as a "report" (given the lack of skills in handwriting, spelling, punctuation and grammar, what chance did I have?)

But the opportunity to put together a story? For an audience? Priceless.

I loved to read. All the time. Always had. Fiction, fiction, fiction. I was one of the kids who had been moved ahead a grade. Reading was more fun than facing kids in the gym who were a year older, six inches taller and thirty pounds heavier.

I put everything I had into that story. Handed it in. Waited for the teacher's reaction. Was delighted that it was the first story he chose to read out loud to the class, announcing ahead of time that I had written it. He finished reading my story—I can still vividly see his face, his long curly hair, his thin nose and round glasses—and he stated it was the stupidest thing he had ever read in all of his years of teaching.

Not making this up.

If I could go back in time, I'd like to tell him about Doc Ivan. I'd let him know that there was a little boy attached to that story. Very attached.

There is a little girl attached to those teeth.

My favorite word in the world is *Daddy,* and you can probably guess one of my emotional reactions to Doc Ivan's answer. Not only was there a little girl attached to those teeth, it was my little girl.

However, along with my gratitude that Doc Ivan cared enough for Olivia to listen to her, I had another emotional reaction: shame.

Decades after grade seven, I still feel the pain of that rejection.

To be human is to tell story. And to tell story is to be human. Our lives are unfolding stories. When we tell stories about our lives, we are sharing ourselves. Because of this, interrupting a child's story indirectly tells the child that the story isn't important. By extension, sadly, this tells the child he or she isn't important.

There is a little girl attached to those teeth.

My shame was in realizing that Doc Ivan had been willing to give Olivia his time and attention, when I, her daddy, had wished to do the opposite. The only reason I hadn't interrupted was because of Doc Ivan's—not Olivia's—importance to me.

But really, if I had cut off my little girl's story, wouldn't I have essentially done to her what my grade-seven teacher did to me?

Once I had a chance to really absorb Doc Ivan's simple answer, I realized how profound it was. I've also realized that his answer speaks very strongly to our efforts to help children become better at reading and writing.

When a student has completed a writing assignment and handed it to you, the first and most important thing to remember is very simple: There is a little boy or girl attached to that story.

For the rest of this book, you'll see that I usually refer to the "little boy." There are a couple of reasons for this. First, it seems that boys need more help with reading and writing than the girls. Second, don't let the size of a boy fool you. He may be in grade ten, six feet tall and playing on the football team, but there's still a little boy somewhere inside. This big boy may pretend he's not hurt by criticism, but it's just pretense. It's the little boy inside who will respond to the slightest bit of real encouragement. I know. I was that boy.

There is a little boy attached to that story.

All the theory about curriculum is irrelevant if we forget that you first need to reach the little boy before he'll absorb what you want to teach, and that the little boy's feelings about how you react to his story matter a great, great deal to the process.

With that in mind, I think it's also important to point out that the attachment has two components.

Yes, as Doc Ivan said, there's a little girl attached to the teeth. Physically, those teeth are important for chewing food. If that's all teeth did, however, parents wouldn't visit Doc Ivan.

Teeth also form a smile.

The emotional component of the little girl attached to those teeth is as important—perhaps more important—than the physical component. When Doc Ivan's prescribed treatment transforms a little girl's crooked teeth into a beautiful smile, he's also transforming that little girl's self-image. It's a huge and enduring emotional lift for the little girl.

It's also an enduring emotional lift for Doc Ivan. I suspect it's one of his biggest motivators. Years after kids have left his treatment, they'll stop him when they see him about town to say hello and share what's happening in their lives.

As a teacher, isn't it amazing to know that you can make an incredible difference in the lives of your students by helping them absorb the knowledge and teachings that will make them feel good about themselves and empower them as adults?

For a little boy and his story, the physical attachment ends the moment he places the paper on your desk or in your hands.

But his emotional attachment is huge.

Truly, we are our stories.

In math or science, being shown our errors isn't as personal as when someone criticizes our story.

Remember: Teeth are more than teeth.

Writing—words on paper—is more than words on paper to be red-marked. Sure, writing is important for delivering information. But words on paper go far past this practicality when they form a story. I say this because far too often in educational settings, *writing* and *story* are used as interchangeable terms.

Let's separate the two. And let's make sure our boys and girls understand the difference too.

This is not much fun:

write a story.

This is way more fun:

write a story.

When we confuse *writing* with *story*, it's vastly more difficult for a student to understand that there is a difference. A critique of the writing mechanics too often feels like a critique of the story itself.

Later, I will talk about focusing on story, involving your students in the process and watching their writing skills blossom. But for now, whether your student has handed in a nonfiction report or a story assignment, it serves you and the student much better to concentrate on the smile instead of on the teeth. In other words, instead of focusing on the writing mechanics, it's better to focus on what the writing is meant to accomplish, which is to deliver story.

To repeat: because we are our stories, a child's emotional attachment to any writing assignment is a crucial factor. I believe that no matter how little effort a student appears to have put into the story, the student has still put a piece of himself into it. Our reaction to that piece of writing has the power to encourage or discourage.

Our reaction to story also forms an emotional connection—positive or negative—with the storyteller.

So, once again, it's about emotional connection. Teacher on one end, student on the other, with both of them firmly attached to the story between them.

CHAPTER 8
TWENTY PERCENT MECHANICS

Because he understands there's a little girl attached to those teeth, Doc Ivan listens to his patients talk about themselves, knowing they will enjoy their time with him. That leads to a strong emotional connection that spills over to the time they devote to caring for their teeth away from his office.

In other words, the five minutes he spent reacting to Olivia's rafting story pays off in a very practical sense. The appointments are six weeks apart, and every night she diligently does the dental maintenance that he has requested, because she feels important to him.

I promise—absolutely promise—that if you show an appropriate emotional reaction to your students' stories, they will happily work hard for you.

Don't believe me?

I've got another story about teeth for you.

Our friends have a seven-year-old son named Adam who was losing a front tooth. It was at the wobbly stage where all that was needed was a quick yank.

Early in an evening I spent with his family, Adam stepped in front of me and pushed on his tooth and waited for my reaction as the tooth bent to almost a 45-degree angle, with just a hint of blood at the root.

I've had my two front teeth knocked out, had twenty-stitch gashes on my leg, endured broken ribs. To tell him that, would have diminished his experience. To shrug off his loose tooth because I've seen worse would have done the same.

I gave him exactly what he wanted. A theatrical wince and a loud groan to let him know how much it was grossing me out. He giggled and ran off to play.

Five minutes later, he did it again: Stood in front me. Pushed on the loose tooth. Out came the same loud groans on my part. Over the next three hours, he and I replayed this scenario at least twenty times.

I know how I could have gotten him to leave me alone. A simple shrug or a yawn when he showed his loose tooth would have done it. Not very fun for him if I don't gasp with horror.

Another example.

When Savannah was five, she would give me shoulder rubs. I didn't critique her method, didn't point out that her fingers weren't strong enough to get through any of my knotted muscles. That would have been the surest way to get her to stop. Instead, I groaned with pleasure each time she put her little fingers on my shoulders, and every night she'd give me another massage.

Appropriate emotional response.

If you want to get kids to stop telling you stories—out loud or on paper—give no positive emotional reaction. Simply point out the mistakes.

On the other hand, if you want more stories, it's just as simple. Gasp, laugh, groan, wince. Let them know their stories are doing something to you.

I promise, you'll be flooded with stories, which means you'll be flooded with writing.

I barely passed high-school English. Nobody to blame but myself.

When my first public story was criticized by that grade-seven teacher, I was devastated. And humiliated. I tell myself now that a teacher who would make such a cruel comment had his own issues, and he deserves my sympathy. So I'm over it. Really.

But I didn't get over it quickly. What I knew from that point on was that I was a failure at all aspects of writing. Not only did he think my story was stupid, he said my handwriting was horrible, my spelling, punctuation and grammar barely passable. I decided that reports were boring because all you did was try to get to the library first to fight for limited copies of the encyclopedia (remember, this was pre-Internet and thus pre-Google). Then you rewrote the facts, making sure you didn't copy word for word. (Boring.) From then on, I had no motivation to write. When you know it's not going to be fun and you don't have a chance at succeeding, why bother trying?

One other thing.

Turns out, much as I loved to read, I wasn't even good at figuring out what stories meant. In my final year of English in high school, I discovered, after reading a class assignment about Helen Keller, that she didn't go to the well for water because she was thirsty. Once again I was corrected in front of the entire class. This time by a crabby female teacher who used a cane to walk back and forth in front of the chalkboard. She archly informed me that Helen Keller did not go to the well because she was thirsty. Water was obviously a symbol for hope, and if I couldn't understand that, I was not very smart. No surprise,

I barely passed the course. Although, in that teacher's defense, I'm sure my attitude inspired her as little as she inspired me.

From grade seven to my third year of university, I had no desire to engage with any kind of writing curriculum.

Doc Ivan has a theory: The process of getting straight teeth is 20 percent mechanics, 80 percent child.

Success is not based solely on his brilliance in orthodontics. While his assessment and prescribed treatment is crucial, he knows the ultimate success depends on the child who needs to follow his instructions, which often takes fifteen or twenty minutes every night before bedtime. He's managed to remove his ego from the process; he doesn't fall into the trap of measuring success by his mastery of how jaws and teeth work.

It's a trap to avoid in education too: the notion that if we teach the right process in the right way, the more successful we will be. That's what curriculum is all about.

Think of all the seminars, classes, courses and lectures meant to help teachers understand and teach curriculum. Think of how curriculum keeps changing course and evolving. Think of how all that focus on curriculum tempts us into near worship of curriculum.

An educational bureaucracy, driven from the top down, says something like this: *If we put a system into place with the right curriculum taught in exactly the right way, then our system is responsible and takes credit for what the child learns, and all we need to do is plug any teacher into that system.*

Instead, what if Doc Ivan's theory—give or take a few percentage points—was applied to teaching? My guess is that if he were a teacher instead of an orthodontist, Doc Ivan's philosophy would be to serve kids first and curriculum second.

His biggest priority would be to understand and connect to the little boy or girl.

When it comes to writing, I think we give too much weight to curriculum because it gives us something black-and-white to teach, and this is easier to do because—unless you understand the magic of great storytelling—story seems mysterious and difficult to teach.

Let's make sure curriculum isn't placed on a pedestal. Let's make it only 20 percent curriculum and 80 percent child. Truly, there's a little boy attached to that story, and your success as a teacher in imparting curriculum won't be determined by the curriculum, but will largely be determined by the little boy and how well you connect with and motivate that little boy.

I know this is true.

Because of one teacher.

CHAPTER 9
ASSEMBLY LINE

I was so horrible at writing, and I hated it so much, that I waited until my third year of college to take the required first-year English course. This teacher I will name. Professor Oppewalle. Calvin College, Grand Rapids, Michigan, late 1970s. Two hundred students in this freshman class. I was one of "them," the kids I see in the gyms at the beginning of my presentations. There only because he has to be. Arms crossed, sullen, not interested in anything anyone has to say about reading and writing.

Our first writing assignment was to describe where we lived. Because I had taken my first two years of college in another city, I had not yet settled in at this college. I wrote about looking for a place to stay, sarcastically describing the joys of using my 1965 Plymouth Valiant, hole in the floorboard and all, as an apartment.

At the beginning of the next class, Professor Oppewalle held up a piece of paper and announced he had found an essay he felt it necessary to share.

In a way, I wasn't surprised when I heard him read aloud the opening paragraphs of my essay. English hated me; I hated English. It made total sense that, once again, I'd be singled out for public criticism.

Professor Oppewalle finished. I can still see his thick, unkempt graying beard and his piercing eyes as he surveyed the room. He told the class that he wasn't going to name the writer so as not to embarrass him. Yeah, small mercy.

But wait.

Professor Oppewalle told the class that he wanted to share the story because he enjoyed the writing and the style and hoped he would see more of the same from the unnamed student who had written this essay.

I wasn't a kid anymore, but really, there was still a little boy attached to that story.

For the rest of that semester, instead of grudgingly throwing something together and expecting a subpar grade, I was determined to live up to Professor Oppewalle's expectations of me. By the end of the semester, I had rediscovered what I'd lost after the savage critique of my first official story at twelve years old: I wanted to write fiction.

Not that getting published came quickly.

Those were the typewriter days. Which meant pounding out—literally—the first draft. I didn't have an electric typewriter. All I could afford—and this was after walking in the snow uphill both directions to school—was a manual Remington in mostly good working order except that the s and z keys needed fishing line to hold the internal levers together, and the fishing line would break every week or so.

Far more important than results was my motivation. I *wanted* to be good. I began red-marking my own stories, determined to make them perfect. Golfers work on their bunker game;

I spent two months mercilessly eradicating any *was* or *is* followed by a verb with an *-ing* ending. Didn't know what grammar thing this was—passive verb, maybe?—just knew that the verb needed to be fresh and immediate and that *was hitting* didn't sound nearly as strong as *hit*. I knew that *smash* or *pound* or *pulverize* were even better words than *hit*, so I'd red-mark that and so on.

~~When I felt I was writing without~~

When I felt I could write without *was* and *-ing*, my next area of attack was redundancies. And so on.

Motivation.

I worked and worked and worked at the fabric of my writing. It meant pulling paper out of the typewriter, finding and circling weaknesses, and retyping. Retyping. Retyping. Seven or eight drafts.

Not that any magazines accepted these much-honed efforts. It didn't help that I started by sending stories to *The New Yorker, Saturday Evening Post, Vanity Fair*. Come on, that's where Hemingway's stories appeared. (Getting a sense that I knew very little about publishing at this point?)

Hundreds and hundreds of pages of writing later, I stopped submitting to the big national magazines and worked down to the medium magazines, and still kept going, refusing to give up on a dream that was sparked by Professor Oppewalle.

Motivation.

It was seven years before my first story was published in *The Western Producer*, a weekly farm supplement for the prairie provinces. Newsprint, not glossy. Didn't matter. I was a published writer with a paycheck of $75 to prove it. It was three more years until I had a book accepted by a publisher.

Motivation.

We can't teach kids to write, any more than we can teach them to skate. Kids teach themselves. We can help them by motivating them to continue. Because there is a little boy attached to every story.

Suggesting there be less emphasis on the intellectual aspect of curriculum is not an attack on curriculum. Nor is it a suggestion that the mechanics of writing have no importance. In Part Four I make an argument for why writing mechanics are absolutely necessary and must be stressed in the teaching process.

But if your first focus is on the little boy or girl, you end up looking for ways to get curriculum to fit the little boy or girl, instead of trying to force the little boy or girl into the curriculum.

Doc Ivan—yes, he's back—calls it an assembly line.

He's aware that he could work that way. He could choose to go quickly from child to child, seeing forty more children a day, two hundred more a week, making decisions based strictly on X-rays and mouth shape, without taking the time to make a connection with each child and without taking time to motivate each boy or girl. Just like an assembly line.

It would be an orthodontic factory. All it needs is an orthodontist plugged into place.

But Doc Ivan knows that is not what is best for the little girl attached to those teeth.

He also knows it's not best for him.

Doc Ivan doesn't want to work on an assembly line. He wants to be a gardener. It gives him much more satisfaction to plant and nurture. While spending 80 percent of his consult getting to know the boy or girl, and only 20 percent on mechanics, is best for the boy or girl, happily enough, it's also best for Doc Ivan.

Remember my reference to all the seminars, classes, courses and lectures out there on how to be better at teaching curriculum material?

Underlying everything is the unspoken pressure on teachers to focus on the student. Learn more, understand the curriculum better, work harder to help the students. It's all about helping the student.

How about a little focus on the teachers? How about more emphasis on making the teaching experience enjoyable?

When bureaucracy pressures teachers to become too focused on curriculum, the danger is that schools become teaching factories. Not much fun or satisfaction for the teachers who are forced to become laborers in a teaching factory.

However, if your first reaction to any piece of writing is to remember that there is a little boy attached, and that curriculum matters far less than how you nurture that boy through the writing process, then the process is going to be just as enjoyable for you as for the boy.

I had a chance, many years after college, to visit Professor Oppewalle and give him a copy of my first two published titles. I told Professor Oppewalle I would never have been published without his simple act of encouragement, and the way he nurtured me and my writing through the rest of the course. It was an awkward, self-conscious moment for me, but he was gracious enough to help both of us overcome it.

A few months after that, back in my hometown of Red Deer, my crabby high-school English teacher, now retired, wasn't as gracious.

I saw her down the aisle in a grocery store, and I made a deliberate detour to where she leaned on her shopping cart, her cane hanging on the handlebar.

I said hello. Her first reaction, with a look of obvious suspicion, was to ask who I was.

I told her my name and then came the payoff.

Her eyes widened, and she said, "Sigmund Brouwer. I remember your name. Didn't I just read about you in the paper? Something about a couple of books published."

I nodded. I waited for her to apologize for how she'd made me suffer in high school, waited for her to admit the short-sightedness, both literal and metaphorical, that had prevented her from recognizing my talent.

"Sigmund Brouwer," she repeated. "Now I remember you in class. A couple of books published? Frankly, I can't believe it."

That was it. She pushed her cart down the aisle and left me standing there.

In retrospect, given how bad my attitude had been all through her class, this reaction was exactly what I deserved.

I now understand that Professor Oppewalle's encouragement would not have been enough without the foundation of writing put into place by all the teachers over the years who endured my bad attitude while I was one of "them," the arms-crossed kids who hate writing.

It's no different than in *The Karate Kid* (original movie) when the main character buffs cars with the famous "wax on, wax off" circular motions. He did it grudgingly, and his teacher would not let him quit, because his teacher knew someday it would pay off.

How did I become a published writer? Through the dedication of teachers who worked hard, with no idea when and how their efforts would make a difference in the lives of any of their students, me among them.

I now understand I should not have walked down the aisle to get an apology from my crabby high-school teacher. Instead, I should have taken the opportunity to thank her.

48

CHAPTER 10
WHEN INFORMATION MATTERS MOST

L et's go back to Dr. Levine's book, *The Myth of Laziness*, which I highly recommend.

In his discourse on the writing process, he succinctly points out what is at stake. While most adults don't need writing skills for essays or stories, he states that "the very fact that writing is so complex justifies its leading role in a curriculum." It meshes brain functions like language, memory and motor control. It is a platform for systematic thinking and problem solving, two abilities that will serve the child extremely well as an adult in any chosen career.

There's more, especially for kids today. A generation earlier, it would have been safe to say that writing skills weren't as important as the systematic thinking and problem-solving skills learned through writing. The Internet, however, has changed this. The ability to write effective emails is crucial for just about every aspect of adult life, and if kids come out of school with the ability to deliver informational writing clearly and concisely, it greatly helps their chances for success.

Pre-Internet, when I applied for a job at the local grocery store at age sixteen, my father stopped me before I left the house and gave me some advice. "Shirt tucked in and hair in place, okay? Shoes tied. Firm handshake and look the manager in the eye as you speak. Don't be afraid to call him sir."

Back then, it was primarily a world of personal contact The Internet hasn't completely eliminated personal contact, but a higher and higher percentage of our communications comes through texting and email. Every day we begin or continue conversations with people we may never meet face-to-face. More often than not, a job application begins with an email, and the look-'em-in-the-eye and firm-handshake opportunity only comes if the online application has made a good impression.

You can make the accurate argument that kids are texters, not emailers, but this underscores the importance of ensuring that kids learn to write proper emails. Texting is for informal social communication, and practice at texting doesn't prepare them for writing emails, which are a necessity for every type of career. Those who are good at writing emails have a far greater chance of success than those who haven't learned the skill, simply because all of us now have to use email a great deal in our working lives.

While my long-term goal is to equip students with the skills to be good at information writing, I wouldn't spend much time, especially early on, directly teaching those skills. Let me explain why.

You love hockey.

The new coach steps into the dressing room for the first practice of the season, surveys you and your friends and all the parents in the room, and says, "Hey, guys. I hope you all agree that to be a great hockey player, you need to be a great skater."

You nod. You know that's true. And you want to be a great hockey player. You are enthusiastic and ready to give your full effort.

"Good," the coach says. "Leave your sticks in the room. We're going to do skating drills for the next hour."

Not so much fun. Especially if the bulk of every practice for the rest of the season means leaving your sticks in the dressing room.

When the final practice of the season is finished, you're a great skater, but you are ready to quit the game. However, you hear that next season this coach will be replaced. You decide to give it another chance.

The new coach steps into the dressing room and like the first one, surveys the players and parents. "Hey, guys. I hope you all agree that to be a great hockey player, you need to be a great skater."

In disgust, you and your friends toss your sticks into the middle of the floor.

This coach frowns. "Guys, what's up?"

"We understand," you say. "Since we need to be great skaters, we need to do more skating drills."

This coach laughs. "Maybe you don't understand."

He takes one puck from the bucket of pucks and holds it up for everyone to see.

"Grab your sticks and follow me."

You go onto the ice. You gather in a circle around this coach. He holds the puck high so that you are all focused on it, then tosses it over your heads, with a simple directive: "Chase it."

"Huh?" a kid beside you says.

Coach grins. "Chase the puck. We have one hour of ice time. Chase it, hold on to it as long as you can and try to score."

All of you wheel around, like a flock of seagulls, and all of you race for the puck. You fight and squawk, first one kid with the puck, then another. The hour flashes past in a chaotic frenzy as you stop, you start, you turn, you fall, you get up, and you keep chasing the puck because it's so much fun. You're gasping for breath as the coach leads the team off the ice, and as you step into the dressing room, you hear one of the parents complain.

"Coach, didn't you say they needed to be great skaters to be great hockey players?"

"Yup."

"But, Coach," the parent says. "An entire hour of ice time. And they didn't do a single skating drill. When are you going to teach the kids how to skate?"

It's not complicated: kids absorbed in the fun of hockey will learn the necessary skills and improve as they play.

Yes, there are times to step in and coach some specifics. Later is often much better than sooner, because the danger in overcoaching is that it will destroy enthusiasm and the motivation that comes with it.

After all, as I said before, we don't teach kids to skate. They teach themselves. By skating.

Our task is to ensure they skate as frequently as possible, as early as possible, allowing them to fall without criticism, allowing them to consciously or unconsciously experiment, allowing them to get lost in the simple act of doing, instead of pulling them out of it again and again by telling them how to do it.

Yes, a skating coach can show a kid how to improve techniques. For kids who already love skating, it's a huge help. But the best skating coach in the world is not going to do much good if early overcoaching has done its damage and the kid only goes through the drills under constant and forced supervision. The same is true for reading and writing.

Somewhere along the way, story too often becomes secondary when it comes to acquiring literacy skills. In short, often we use the writing process—the mechanics—to teach writing, when the fun part is story. That would be like using skating drills to teach skating, when the fun part is hockey.

Since we are so wired to respond to story, make story the engine. If your literacy focus with kids is predominantly on story—not on reading or writing—your students have a much better chance of learning reading and writing skills as a result. Just as kids learn to skate by playing hockey.

When story is the primary focus, kids learn to read. They don't care if they miss every fifth or sixth word, because story compels them to move forward, makes them want to reach the end to find out what happens. And after that story, they'll read another and another and another, and soon enough, so gradually they don't notice it happening, they won't miss every fifth or sixth word.

When story is the primary focus, kids learn to write as a byproduct of using words to put that story down on paper. Especially if they are rewarded for their stories by your positive emotional reaction.

The key, then, is to make sure kids still have fun putting stories on paper. And I guarantee the fastest way to shut down a kid's enthusiasm for putting stories down on paper is to point out what's wrong instead of celebrating what's great.

Yes, yes, yes. The end goal is for kids to become competent at information writing. And yes, yes, yes, information writing may serve them much better as adults than the ability to put stories on paper. So yes, yes, yes, in the end, information writing is crucial.

But allowing them to have fun with story in their playground years is the best way to give them those information-writing skills as adults.

So, really, isn't story everything?

CHAPTER 11
THE GENDER DIFFERENCE

Here's a typical story, written by a grade-three boy, almost guaranteed to result in frustration for boy and (usually female) teacher/parent:

The dog chased the cat. The cat ran up the tree. The dog barked for a while. The cat stayed in the tree. The dog went home. The end.

Boys read the story and have a single-word reaction: *Cool*.

That's my reaction too. Because this was written by an eight-year-old, I'm not expecting the story to be infused with emotional complexity. Although it's barely over twenty-five words, I don't see it as a bad story. It's clear. It starts with a problem, the problem gets worse, the problem is resolved.

When he's older and capable of handling more, that's a different situation. But for a kid who has only been writing for a couple of years, I wouldn't ask for much more. Except maybe another story, since my premise is that kids get better at writing by writing. As I mentioned earlier, if the goal is to get him to write a hundred words, I'd rather see four stories of twenty-five words happily written, than grinding the poor kid to add seventy-five words to a story that he thought was complete.

But then, I'm a guy.

Say I'm at the gym with my buddy Craig. We're doing bench presses. He's standing nearby as I struggle to push up 300 pounds. (Yes, that's definitely exaggerating. But, given the gender issue we're discussing, not only do we need a stereotypically manly situation, but I might as well portray myself as extremely manly. If, of course, bigger muscles is the definition of manhood, which of course, we all agree it's not.)

Anyway, there I am, dripping with manly sweat, about to heave the last rep of 300 pounds skyward, and Craig says, "Looks like me and Sherri are going to get divorced."

Kindly, I do not point out his bad grammar. Instead, I say, "Oh," as I push against the barbell.

Noting my manly exhaustion, he says, "Need a spot with the weights?"

I grunt, "Yes."

He helps me finish the last rep. End of conversation.

When I get home, I courteously pass on this information, because I know my wife will appreciate hearing it.

"Honey," I say, "I was at the gym with Craig. He and Sherri are getting a divorce."

(Note the perfect grammar.)

"What?" she says. "Craig and Sherri?"

"Yes," I say with love and patience, "Craig and Sherri are getting a divorce."

"Craig and Sherri," she says. "A divorce."

Model husband that I am, I don't point out that I am repeating myself. "Divorce. Hey, want me to start the barbecue? I'm starving."

"Why?" she says.

"It was a great workout," I answer, flexing my biceps. "Can you see a difference already?"

"No," she says, ignoring the manly display. "Why are they getting a divorce?"

"Don't know," I say. "We've got some steak in the fridge, right?"

"You didn't ask Craig why they are getting a divorce?"

Of course I didn't. If he wanted me to know, he would have told me.

She continues. "How does Craig feel about this?"

"Don't know," I say. "Never asked." I mean, if he'd wanted to tell me, he would have.

"I have to call Sherri," she says.

"Sure. I'll start the grill." Then I catch the way she's looking at me. "Now you're mad at me?"

Wow, didn't see that coming. Even after years of being a model husband.

Neither does the innocent and hapless boy who has just turned in his story: **The dog chased the cat. The cat ran up the tree. The dog barked for a while. The cat stayed in the tree. The dog went home. The end.**

Some of the homeschool mothers I've worked with would have questions about this story.

What was wrong in the relationship between the dog and the cat? And couldn't this be solved without the dog resorting to intimidation that resulted in the cat seeking refuge?

How did the dog feel when it could not reach the cat?

When the dog finally gave up and went home, did it share its frustration with its friends?

At this point, editorial help is no longer about writing. It's going to consist of pulling all these details out of this poor kid, who had no idea this minefield was in front of him or that he was going to be forced to make up stuff to add to the story.

Which makes it no longer his story, but the adult's.

Which also makes him leery about writing another story.

First, from his perspective, he's never going to get the story right. And second, he's going to face the same kind of grilling when he hands in the next one.

Not much motivation there.

Much better, I believe, to read the story and say instead: "Yikes. I was pretty afraid for that cat. Good thing it survived. Got a story about elephants next?"

"I'm always hopeful that sports will
be enough of a draw in a story to
grab the reluctant readers."

I LOVE TAKING MY daughters to see a new movie in a theater. There's the popcorn, the great sound, the big screen. And there is the expectation of entertainment through story.

When *Shrek 4* came out, it was a high priority on our movie list. As our entire family settled into our seats, it occurred to me that nobody teaches "movie watching."

However, with the opening film credits rolling, I wondered how kids might react to watching a movie if they were forced to analyze it, write a report about it, then have their mistakes pointed out to them, get a grade on the report, and finally face parents who might criticize them for not getting a good enough grade. How much longer would movies be fun?

Next I wondered what would happen if we taught kids hockey by sitting them down in front of a television to watch classic games—like the 2010 Winter Olympics final where Canada won the gold medal—and forced them to analyze various breakout patterns, write a report about it, have their mistakes pointed out to them, get a grade on the report, and finally face parents who might criticize them for not getting a good enough grade. How much longer would hockey be fun?

I was thinking of all of this just before Shrek roared into life on the screen. When he appeared, I stopped thinking about it completely. The story had me hooked.

PART 3

WRITE STORY

CHAPTER 12

MOTIVATION

Kids learn to write by writing. Curriculum is there to guide us and to provide educators with the appropriate levels or expectations.

In my ideal world of education, we would teach kids the curriculum points through curriculum exercises, and allow them to teach themselves through their own writing.

In other words, when they are at the grade level to learn capitalization, give them capitalization exercise sheets and apply the discipline there, backing off when it comes to putting stories on paper.

Most hockey practices are like this. There are sets of organized drills to prepare the players for game situations, and the coaches supervise these drills closely, making sure the players are learning the mechanics. But when it comes to playing the game, coaches don't step in and blow the whistle and correct mechanical errors. The game flows and the coaches can only watch, offering advice between shifts.

This is why I don't worry too much about supervising story writing. In essence, I tell the kids what they need to accomplish, then let them have fun figuring out how to accomplish it.

What's important is that first I understand story well enough to give the overview advice, and that they, in turn, understand the broader picture.

No different from hockey. Coaches who understand the game help players understand the game, but the players themselves make it happen within those parameters.

The simpler the parameters, the more freedom the kids have. The more freedom, the more fun. The more fun, the more words they put on paper. The more words they put on paper, the better they get at writing.

When I looked at some books on helping kids write, I found that often there is so much advice on the details of the process that it's difficult to see the simple parameters.

Because of that, I offer students only three broad principles for how to get their audience to react emotionally to a story.

1. Daydream the story.
2. Structure the story.
3. Use words to make pictures.

I know this works. My writing seminars have up to forty students, with writers from grades three to twelve. Their writing and reading skills range from extremely reluctant to excellent. Despite this mix, four hours fly by.

Because once the writers understand the three principles, if I've motivated them properly, they will work at their own pace, according to their own skill level.

And they come up with great stories. Some are very short stories, with a lot of misspelled words. But they are stories that we celebrate.

I'm convinced that if we focus on the fun of story, the writing and spelling will improve. It's very gratifying to return to a town for a follow-up seminar a year later and hear from parents that their kids' writing has improved, simply through the practice of putting story on paper.

The three basic principles of putting story on paper can be applied to all curriculum techniques. In other words, the three basics supply the concept, and your specific curriculum builds on that concept.

Remember Dr. Levine's description of the writing process in his book *The Myth of Laziness*?

I'm in total agreement with him on how complicated it is. I'm also in total agreement with anyone who describes all the different processes and motor skills and neural connections it takes to walk. Truly, once you analyze what it takes to remain balanced and upright while you move forward as a biped, it sounds so complicated as to be almost impossible. But we are genetically wired to be able to put one foot in front of another, even while going down a set of stairs, carrying an uneven load. We have been given the mental and physical tools to make it simple.

If we keep the structure of story simple, kids can figure out the rest themselves. That's why I think motivating students is more important than trying to teach them the mechanics. I'm much more concerned about passing along "why" to write, than "how" to write.

And keeping the instructional part as simple as possible is going to make it easier on you and your students.

CHAPTER 13

DAYDREAMS
AND RESEARCH

A teacher once told me about his biggest moment of horror and shock. He and his brother grew up on a farm. In the middle of a boring summer, they hauled a sledgehammer and a couple of fenceposts to the edge of an open pasture. They pounded the fenceposts into the ground about six feet apart, then cut through six bicycle tire tubes to make long rubber bands, which they attached to the fenceposts to create a giant slingshot.

Wouldn't be much of a story if they hadn't used it.

No, when you have a giant slingshot, you need to try it out.

They grabbed a rock the size of a baseball and fired it, wondering how far it might go into the pond in front of them.

The slingshot was far more powerful than they expected. The teacher described how the rock flew over the pond and headed straight toward some cows grazing on the hillside.

In the gym, when I retell this, do you think the little boys in the gym are listening?

You bet.

In real life, that rock hit a cow in the head and the cow fell over sideways and remained motionless on the ground. The teacher was convinced the rock had killed the cow and that his father would ground them for infinity. Fortunately, for both beast and boys, after about five minutes, the cow slowly got up and resumed grazing.

I use this story to make a point about the importance of daydreaming to writing. I invite the kids in the gym to daydream with me.

What if, instead of hitting a cow in the head, the rock hit a bull...?

No! What if you built a slingshot that big in your backyard, and instead of firing a rock, you decided to catapult a big poopy diaper? And what if the diaper opened as it went through the air...?

I extend my full sympathy to teachers who find nothing amusing about the image of an open diaper sailing over the man in the yard next door, who is innocently grilling some burgers and saying, "Honey, I don't remember putting any corn in the salad."

Yet.

I use the slingshot story as a way to convey the concept of incorporating daydreaming into writing. I hope those same teachers understand that if I can emotionally engage the boys in the gym, especially the ones who don't read much, they just might go back to the classroom and write their own story, or at the least, read *Long Shot*, the book I wrote based on my own daydreams about a diaper—er, rock—sailing through the air.

If good stories make the audience feel something, then it's a very helpful principle to keep in mind during the research stage of writing anything, fiction or otherwise. I advise kids to research not only for facts, but to also be on the lookout for anything that pushes their emotional buttons. There's a good chance that those things will push their readers' emotional buttons too.

Research can be a tedious process, especially when books simply relay facts, without the context of story. I'm always amazed when I read—too frequently—dull history books. History is a collection of stories about people who fought through and either conquered or were defeated by problems. History is STORY. As a result, history books should be riveting. But when they are not, I'm prepared to go through twenty pages of tediousness, looking for the one gold nugget that I can retell.

When I wrote my adult novel *The Last Disciple*, I decided that since the bulk of my readers would be women, a childbirth scene would have immediate emotional impact. I remembered the nurses' scorn when I fell asleep while my wife was in labor. How much more furious would women readers be at a man who pushes aside the midwives and begins berating his wife during the final contractions? It was my intent that women readers would be so angry at him, they would be compelled to keep reading, hoping he would die a slow painful death.

I then raised the emotional stakes. At the opening of the novel, when the woman won't do as the husband demands during this tirade, he gives her an ultimatum: *Do as I tell you to do, or we will not name the child. Do as I tell you, or the slave will take away this child and let it die of exposure.* The woman passes out from blood loss before she can answer. In the next scene, readers see the baby alone in a temple courtyard, abandoned to die of cold beneath a statue of Nero.

Again, I was hoping that the readers could not put the book down. I was also hoping that when the main character appears in the book and decides to ignore the Roman traditions I researched so carefully and rescue the baby, readers would immediately like him, and that this emotional connection would propel them forward as the main character cares for the child.

Because I believe that stories connect emotionally, it's probably pretty transparent how I try to engage the kids through my presentations. I'm simply retelling stories that made me feel something: happy or grossed-out or afraid or angry.

Research becomes a lot more fun if you can daydream while you do it.

And daydreaming situations for fiction is even more fun.

Watching the *Discovery Channel* one evening with Olivia, we were both mesmerized by a show on sharks. Talk about pushing emotional buttons! Each segment of the show drew us in by evoking curiosity, fear or fascination.

The format of each segment followed classic story form. It posed a problem, showed how scientists had struggled to find the answer and then presented the solution.

With hammerhead sharks, for example, we learned that because the eyes are set on each end of the "hammer," these sharks have excellent depth perception. But because a hammerhead shark's jaw is so far below its eyes, when the shark gets directly above its prey, it loses sight of the prey.

Scientists began to experiment to find out how the hammerhead manages to locate, say, a shrimp. Wondering if the shark could sense electromagnetic currents, scientists buried a nail under sand in the water, then ran a light current through it. When the current hit the nail, the shark attacked.

Fascinating.

That still didn't explain where this ability came from. In the end, Olivia and I learned that hammerhead sharks have a special gel in certain glands near their throats. This gel gives them a sensitivity to electricity that is about 20,000 times greater than other sharks.

Not only fascinating, but because it was presented in story form, also very satisfying.

Falling asleep that night, I was struck by a thought: What if there were humans who possessed heightened sensitivity to electromagnetism?

Then I had a really weird thought: What if these humans could detect electromagnetic changes in other humans possessed by demons?

The novel is now out. It's called *The Canary List*.

CHAPTER 14
STORY STRUCTURE

S ometimes I think literary analysis and curriculum make things too complicated. It all comes down to only two words:

Poop happens.

CHAPTER 15

SERIOUSLY, WHAT IS STORY STRUCTURE?

Okay. Three words:

Problem. Worse. Solved.

CHAPTER 16
STORY'S ENGINE

It would be insincere if I apologized for the previous two chapters and the cryptic kung-fu-master approach to story.

Happy to justify it though.

I'm hoping my deliberate succinctness will be memorable. Especially in comparison to material that makes story unnecessarily complicated.

Story is not complicated. Stories themselves range from simple to complex, but the concept of story is very simple. It is a series of events, but not just events like a cloud passing in front of the sun or a dog running through a field. Without a problem—some people call it conflict—none of these scenes are story.

If you pushed me and asked me for a lengthier explanation, I'd go as high as five words: Poop happens; then it stops.

There's nothing more you really need to understand about story structure.

Even though our lives are unfolding stories, in order to satisfy an audience, story needs to have a degree of structure that is not always completely realistic. Tragically, too many of our own problems or the problems of the people we care about do not have a satisfactory resolution. In story, we have a strong emotional need for resolution, perhaps to make up for the capriciousness of life.

To repeat: Without a problem, there is no story.

How important is this?

Great writers make sure that every scene or chapter has an inherent conflict.

How important is this?

Venerable screenwriter Hal Ackerman requires all his students in his graduate screenwriting class at UCLA to sign a contract: *I solemnly swear that in every screenplay I write, every scene will have woven into its architecture the element of CONFLICT.*

They are permitted to write a scene without conflict only after successfully applying for exception through another document called the "Application for Waiver of Conflict."

Important as conflict is, however, and much as a story can be reduced to the simplicity of problem-worse-solved, the power of story doesn't come from its structure. It comes from our emotional reaction to the unfolding problems and subsequent solution.

A cloud passing over the sun is not a story. When a cloud passing over the sun threatens to become a tornado funnel that could strike a family in their camper on vacation, we care.

A rabid dog in a field is not a story. When a rabid dog chases a little girl through a field, we care.

When an orphan girl is alone at a train station, waiting for her adoptive family to arrive, we care. Especially when we discover that Mr. Cuthbert wanted a boy, not a girl.

Story's form (problem-worse-solved) is not the same as formula. In formulaic fiction, all the plots and characters are similar.

While that has a comfortable familiarity, it can also become stale quite quickly.

Recognizing structure and assessing a story or report using structure makes it easier to coach kids as they work on story. If I'm working with a student who can't seem to get past half a page, I ask him to daydream the problem getting worse. But if I'm working with a student who spends pages and pages of writing without advancing the story, I get that student to focus on the resolution of the problem.

CHAPTER 17

HIDE THE THUMB

Every time I talk to students about starting a story with *who, what, where* and *when,* I show them the back of my hand with all four fingers spread as wide as possible. I tick off each finger as I recite the four Ws. Index finger for the *who* and so on.

As I speak, I make sure my thumb is folded down into my palm, effectively hiding it from their view, so that all they see are those four fingers.

Without exception, someone blurts out another word: *why.*

This student, like most kids, has been taught to start a story with all five Ws.

It's an interruption that I welcome and wait for, because it gives me the opportunity to suggest a different way of looking at writing a story.

Yes, the fingers and thumb are all connected to the hand.

Yes, all five are necessary for a hand to work properly.

But the thumb looks different from the fingers. The thumb has a different role.

That's why I keep it hidden as I make my point.

Who and *where* and *when* and *what* are the elements that put a picture in a reader's head.

Barney, the big fat purple dinosaur, was at the playground on a summer morning. He began to climb the flagpole.

That's all we need to form a picture.

To advance the story, though, we need to ask a question like *Why?* or *What next?* That question is the thumb.

Putting it as simply as possible: 1) hide the thumb while you create a picture by using the four fingers; 2) hook your readers by popping up the thumb; that's when things get really interesting; and 3) have fun making the problem worse and worse until you solve it.*

---

*A short video at rockandroll-literacy.com explains this in a different way.

IN THE SUMMER, when the kids don't have to get up early for school, my wife Cindy and I enjoy a couple of cups of tea together on the back deck. One morning we were discussing this book, and I told her that one of the main points I wanted to make was that while the intellectual component of writing was extremely important, the emotional component has to come first, because story connects us and we get lost in stories because of how stories make us feel.

"Oh," she said, "you mean write from the heart, and edit from the brain?"

Her casual brilliance was so irritating that I had to fight the temptation to steal the phrase and present it as my own.

But it is hers, and I'm not sure it can be any more succinct than that.

Write from the heart, and edit from the brain.

PART 4
REVISE STORY

CHAPTER 18

NEVER WRITE
BEYOND THE HEADLIGHTS

"Writing is like driving at night in the fog. You can only see as far as your headlights, but you can make the whole trip that way."
—E.L. Doctorow

After twenty years of publishing novels, I've come to a point where I truly understand Doctorow. I got there the hard way. A few years ago, I had decided, after fifteen published novels, that I'd better learn something about novel structure. I thought that if I structured a novel before writing it, the novel would be better and it would be easier to write. Instead, writing the next three novels using this method was hellish for me. Long, long struggles as I tried to fit my character's journeys into a predetermined plan. (If I were smarter, it would have only taken one novel to realize this.)

Finally, I reviewed the first fifteen novels that I'd written "haphazardly" and realized they had all fallen, more or less, within the same structures I used when I tried to plan a novel. At that point, I decided that with the current novel, *Realm,*

I would no longer try to write smart and efficient. I was going to throw all of that away and wing it again, with all the optimism and ignorance I'd brought to my first novels. I'd start with a character in a situation and, day by day, chapter by chapter, see where his actions took him.

I wasn't going to write past the headlights.

While I can't see an entire novel unfold in my head, I have much less difficulty coming up with a single scene. It's not even that the entire scene happens at once, just that I can juggle the five or six action points and keep them in my head until I begin putting them on paper.

For example, in *Realm*, chapter four, I began by visualizing a scene, with the goal of coming up with an event (perhaps random, perhaps not) that would save the life of my main character, a homeless man named Crockett who had once been an emergency-room physician. Since the subject of the book was demons and angels, I wanted a realistic and yet ambiguous scene that would cause him (and the reader) to wonder if what happened had been divine intervention or simply coincidence.

I imagined a newspaper, flung by a gust of wind, distracting him long enough to stop him in his tracks, thus preventing his death. Then I wondered how that could save his life. Hmmm. One more step and a piano drops on him? No, too clichéd and too unlikely. Okay, he's walking down the street. What could kill him? Then I visualized a texting driver swerving onto the sidewalk. Also, since this was early in the novel, I wondered if I could also use this scene to show the reader who Crockett had been in his previous life. An immediate answer came to me. Yes, a gust of wind throws the paper in his face. Crockett stops short. A car misses him by inches as it crosses the sidewalk and crashes through a storefront window. The texting driver's life is in danger; Crockett reluctantly steps in with his first-aid experience.

I distrust the easy answers. If it's that obvious to me, it's also obvious to the reader, and as a result, less fun. It's the unpredictable that I enjoy when I'm reading a novel. Unpredictable but also plausible.

I played the entire scene out in my head, trying out different variations until I saw something that was unexpected yet plausible.

I visualized the woman behind the steering wheel after crashing the car. Broken glass had punctured her neck. In panic, she pulls it loose and blood pumps from an artery. She's got maybe a minute to live unless the wound is effectively plugged. Crockett opens the car door and searches the contents of the woman's purse, looking for something to stem a deep wound. Which meant that I, too, had to scrabble through the (imagined) contents of the woman's purse. Weird as it sounds, I went over to my wife's purse (with her permission!) and began searching for items that might be helpful in a car accident.

Hand sanitizer. Good for making sure Crockett's grubby hands wouldn't cause infection. But with a puncture wound, the blood would be gushing so fast that infection might not be the biggest issue. So Crockett sees the hand sanitizer but doesn't waste time using it. Then I saw a wrapped tampon in my wife's purse. Crazy, I told myself, but the more I thought about it, the more logical it seemed. Still, maybe too crazy, even for me. I went to a writer's best friend: Google. I typed in four words: *tampon as emergency bandage*. I discovered that army field medics have been using tampons to staunch bullet wounds for years, leaving a plug outside the wound for surgeons to access later. Bingo. Unexpected, yet plausible.

As I wrote that scene, I gave no further thought to the next events of the novel, and certainly not to the remaining 250 to 300 pages. After the difficulties of the previous three novels, no longer was I going to write beyond my headlights.

The next day, however, when I began the process all over again, I was now aided by a new jumping-off point, one I had never expected when I began the car-accident scene, let alone when I wrote the first sentence of the novel.

I began to think about a homeless guy who saves a woman's life in an unusual way, then leaves the accident scene, wanting to remain anonymous. Is he going to get away with this? Or did someone record the scene on a cell phone? Does the media get the video? What happens as people start looking for him? I decided to follow my headlights through a new set of curves, and began visualizing the next scene.

In short, as an adult with writing experience, my headlights allow me to juggle the events of an entire scene in my head. I've learned the hard way that trying to imagine the entire novel most often leads to paralysis.

As it turned out, a third of the way into the novel, I threw most of it away. I didn't like where it was headed. I asked myself instead who a girl might turn to for help if she can't depend on her parents.

Gone was that entire scene of a car accident. Gone was a homeless man who had once been an emergency doctor. Gone, too, was the title.

That book became *The Canary List*. And the one person who has the compassion and courage to help the girl is a school-teacher named Crockett Grey.

I think the "driving within the headlights" analogy is accurate, and especially relevant to kids and writing, but with one key difference: their headlight beams show much less of the road ahead.

Around the time I finished the car-accident scene, Savannah faced a first-grade writing assignment that was causing her a lot of frustration. She had been given a list of words and needed to write six sentences, each one containing a word from the list. The six sentences had to fit together to form a story.

I don't mind it when either of my girls has to face difficulties. Overcoming difficulties independently is a way to learn and to build confidence. I believe I do them a disservice by stepping in, especially before they ask for help. One of the big phrases in our household—okay, one of *my* big phrases—is this: Figure it out for yourself.

Savannah was at the point of tears, though, so I sat down beside her and let her explain to me what she needed to do. She told me she couldn't think of a story and that she just couldn't do the exercise.

I asked her if she could choose one word and put it into a sentence. That came very easily to her. She pointed at *children* on the vocab list and blurted out, "Our family has **children**."

I wrote it down for her because my handwriting is faster, and I didn't want her creative process blocked by painfully slow mechanics. The sentence was on paper for her. She read it back to herself, and it took about ten seconds for the next sentence to follow:

*They went into a **barn**.*

A few seconds later: *They saw a kitten playing with **yarn**.*

Ten more seconds: *Mommy walked in pushing a **cart**.*

A few more seconds: *She walked **by** the kittens.*

Then about twenty seconds for a wrap-up: *The kittens were not doing any **harm**.*

Savannah was now excited about her story. By staying within the headlights, her entire journey had been a process of discovery, not anxiety.

Creativity is a mysterious process and probably, by definition, a journey of the unexpected. It builds upon itself. Thinking of one thing leads to another and then another. When you get to the end, you can look back and see a logical progression, but like driving down the road at night, you never see beyond the headlights and you don' t understand where the journey is taking you until you've arrived.

CHAPTER 19
WRITING IS DIFFICULT

In a gymful of students, I'll often ask how many find writing difficult. Nearly all the kids put their hands up. I express jealousy at the kids who find writing easy, and tell all the others that there are days I'd rather thump my forehead with a dictionary than write another sentence.

For most of us, writing is difficult.

I think it's important to establish that truth early and often with students.

First, when students are unaware that just about everyone else struggles with writing, they think their own silent difficulties mean they aren't smart.

In sports, it's much easier to understand that the struggle is shared. Look around the bunny slopes at a ski hill and you'll see that everyone else is falling down as frequently as you are. Not so in writing. The classroom is silent, all heads are bowed, and you are in your private world of misery, worsened because you believe everyone else is flying along.

Writing is difficult.

Once you understand that writing is difficult, it becomes less difficult. Because you have adjusted your expectations.

In his book *The Road Less Traveled*, Dr. M. Scott Peck makes the same point about life. If we believe it's supposed to be easy, we'll always be resentful that it's difficult, and this resentment adds to the difficulty. Those of us who realize life is about solving one problem and moving on to the next bring a different attitude to the situation, which makes life easier.

Intellectually, this makes sense.

I understood it emotionally a few months after reading Dr. Peck's book. I was visiting a friend one summer at Lake Michigan. He said he needed the spark plugs changed on his boat, and, as the son of a mechanic, I volunteered.

He lifted the flooring of the deck to expose the twin engines, and I struggled for two hours to reach and change all sixteen spark plugs.

Back home in Alberta, hanging out with my dad at his automotive repair shop, I told him about this incident and mentioned that he was lucky he worked on cars, not boats. He said it wouldn't matter. With the indignation of experience, I informed him that it would take two hours to change spark plugs on a boat, compared with fifteen minutes on an old V-8. He shook his head sadly at my lack of wisdom and said, "Son, I'd expect it to take two hours."

Aaaah.

Life is difficult. Recognize this, and life is no longer as difficult.

Writing is difficult. Allow the kids to recognize this, and it won't frustrate them nearly as much.

And let's remember too, that physically, writing is difficult for some kids. They are accustomed to talking effortlessly and can deliver verbal stories with verve. But the process of scratching out words on paper, letter by letter, is not easy, especially for younger ones. To get a sense of this difficulty, write alongside them, but write with your non-dominant hand.

Mentally, too, writing drains you.

In my workshops, I rarely get the kids to write for more than twenty minutes at a time. I know how wearing it can be. In my own office, I'll work intensely for twenty minutes or so, then give myself a break—another cup of coffee, a quick game of solitaire, a few minutes with my putter and a couple of golf balls. Then back to the computer.

In all-day workshops, I intersperse writing periods with stand-and-stretch breaks where kids play Rock-Paper-Scissors until someone gets a prize for surviving to the end. Other times, it will be a paper-airplane contest, as one by one they throw their own creations across the room, with the plane that goes the farthest winning a prize. The games get them talking and buzzing, energized for another round of writing. Soon enough, they understand any writing they do will be rewarded with some fun, and getting them to focus becomes easier and easier.

CHAPTER 20
TEACHING REVISION

Before I start, let me be clear: Revision is self-editing. Editing is usually something done to your work by someone else.

I'd been asked to work with some kids on revisions for a couple of days. Sounded easy over the phone. Then I got to the school and discovered I would be facing a tough grade-eight inner-city class.

I worked hard to make an immediate emotional connection by telling a few stories. I was pleased when the kids laughed at my rants about spelling, adverbs and redundancies. But I couldn't see any way to keep the connection when it came to getting them to look critically at their own writing. All the crossed arms that had come uncrossed would cross again as soon as I asked them to self-edit.

I don't know where the inspiration came from—do we ever?—but I decided something else might work better.

I had my laptop with me, so I explained that I was going to do something I'd never done before: I was going to publicly share a piece of unedited work. I told them I had no idea whether it was any good, and that I was worried they might not like it. I asked for their kindness ahead of time. Then I explained that after I read the piece out loud, I was going to ask for their help to make it better.

With that rambling setup, I read them the first chapter of *Crown of Thorns*. A girl named Angel is in a cemetery at night, instructing two men on how to dig a grave for a body that she wants hidden in plain sight—among all the other dead. When I finished reading, I asked the class to tell me which parts were unclear or boring. Not *if* there were any parts unclear or boring.

Silence.

I had to ask three times before a girl put up her hand. She was hesitant but suggested that something in the first paragraph didn't make sense.

I could have reacted defensively. I could have told her I was a published writer and she wasn't, and that I knew what I was doing and she didn't. That would have guaranteed no more comments from the class.

Instead, I reread the first paragraph and asked her if she had any suggestions that might fix it. Then, with all the kids watching me at my laptop, I typed in her suggestions, reread the paragraph and asked if that had fixed it.

She was grinning as she said yes. At that point, I knew my spur-of-the-moment tactic was working. Especially because four other students now had their hands up.

As a group, we spent nearly forty minutes reworking that first chapter. Most of the time I agreed with their suggestions. Occasionally, I'd explain why I needed something to stay the way it was. I hoped I was succeeding in showing that words are tools with specific functions, and that revising is not about being wrong. It's about making a piece of writing stronger.

For the rest of that workshop, whenever I worked with an individual student, the boy or girl wasn't the least bit defensive about discussing or changing his or her writing.

Whenever you are trying to get across a new curriculum concept to your students, if you can make your own writing the first focus of improvement, it's going to make it a lot easier when you work with students on theirs.

Put in some deliberate and glaring mistakes. That makes it a lot more fun for them to catch and correct.

I learned a method of reviewing from a great teacher; she calls it "Two Stars and a Wish." Whether she's doing the reviewing or it's peer reviewing, rule number one is that the comments are not written directly on the story or report. Instead, everyone in her class uses sticky notes. Comments are limited to three. Two of the sticky notes are compliments with handwritten stars across the top. The third sticky note is a "wish" for a specific something to be different.

Try it. It works.

Time and again, I run into parents who make sure that their kids rewrite their stories and reports so that they are handing in a "good" copy.

They do this because that's what they were taught, back in the day.

But rewriting in "good" is not about improving writing, it's about improving handwriting. First off, handwriting skills were a lot more important before computers arrived. Second, handwriting is drudgery. Writing is difficult enough for kids. Let's take as much drudgery out of it as possible.

Writing should be about learning to use words to tell a story. How you get the story onto paper isn't what's important. Kids struggle with the mechanics of handwriting at the best of times. Their brains work much faster than their hands and pencils. I'm in favor of having kids dictate their stories, either to parents or into a microphone using a software program like Dragon Dictation. When they see the crisp fonts on their printout, it's inspiring for them. And once the words are on paper, they can revise freely.

I suggest getting kids to triple-space the first draft of every story. That makes it a lot easier to add marks and corrections and extra words.

I suggest asking them to revise only one out of five stories.

I suggest that once they are finished revising—if it's hand-written—they don't have to rewrite in "good." The important thing is to learn the revision process. Why de-motivate a kid by punishing him with a handwriting exercise after he's finished his revisions?

"It's amazing how creative the stories are
when kids don't worry about making mistakes."

MECHANICS

WORDS

STORY

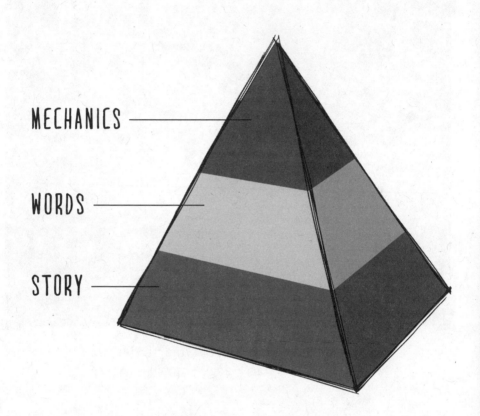

CHAPTER 21
THE WRITING PYRAMID

Quick, what's the most important part of a pyramid?

I love it when someone in the writing class blurts out, "The tip."

Most of us immediately assume it's the foundation. After all, without a foundation, the pyramid is weak. If you try to rest a pyramid on its tip, it falls over.

So, the most important part of a pyramid is the foundation.

But really, the most important part is the tip. Without a tip, it doesn't look like a pyramid. Take away the tip and it might remain solid and in place for thousands of years, but no one is going to call it a pyramid.

Using that same line of reasoning, the middle part of the pyramid is actually the most important.

Yeah, yeah, easy to figure out where this is going. Each part of the pyramid is the most important part.

With the kids, once we've agreed upon this, I add a little more to the pyramid.

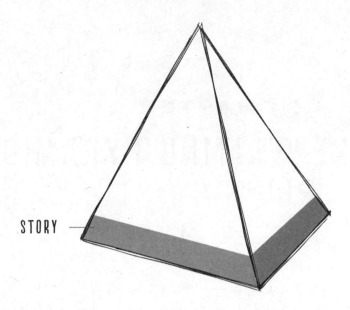

STORY

Build your writing by making story the foundation. After all, a good story told with plain words and bad grammar is still much more interesting than a boring story with poetic language and perfect grammar and spelling.

But if you have a great story, I say, take it to the next level by using great words and great description.

And when you're finished with that (if someone else is going to read it) make sure you complete the appearance of your story—the tip of the pyramid—with good spelling, proper punctuation and correct grammar.

CHAPTER 22

PYRAMID BASE: REVISING STORY

The base of my writing pyramid is, of course, story. When I discuss revisions with the kids, I always start with revising story, because too often they think all they need to worry about is checking their spelling and punctuation.

But story revision is the most crucial, because story is the foundation. And often, story revision is the most difficult aspect.

Seven months of work to complete my first draft of *The Canary List*. Then a three-week wait until I received my first comments from my editor.

Sigmund:
Things I like about the book:
- *Interesting concept—women who can sense demons due to special sensitivity in electromagnetism embedded in* DNA.
- *Exploring the modern church's lack of interest in the supernatural.*
- *Crockett's brokenness about his daughter's death.*

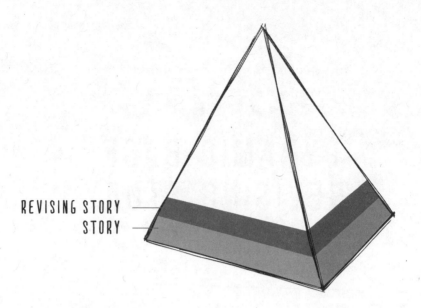

REVISING STORY
STORY

- O'Hare's confession to Crockett at end—all for personal gain. Good twist.

Things I didn't like:

- Crockett. He is an obnoxious jackass who presents himself as much less intelligent than he is because he can only communicate with other humans through vague, not-so-witty banter.
- The women characters. They were all bitchy or slutty or both. Very male presentation of them and surprisingly shallow.
- First third of the book concentration on Crockett and his problems that feels very out-of-balance with back end of book and the Vatican adventures.
- Lack of reason to sabotage Crockett's life by any party. Lack of reason that the "good guys" at the Vatican should help him out. Lack of reason to become "spiritually sensitive" at end.

- *Book almost all Crockett POV—who isn't likable and keeps reader from processing the understanding of events because a) his own limited understanding and b) discoveries are primarily communicated through circular banter than is wearisome and confusing.*
- *Loads of potential with the genealogy search and bringing in the "list" idea earlier but not explored.*
- *Jamie has character potential but is wasted in the pawn role. She disappears for more than half the book. And technically she is the one they are really after. And 10 is too young. 12?*
- *Guy who repeats himself, Catfish's pot habit, the encroaching friend of the family making a move on the ex—feels devicey and overcooked. Reader rolls eyes.*

After all of this, my editor wrote: *And now for the big problems with the manuscript...*

You might think my feelings were hurt.

Not a chance. First, she knows I don't want things sugared-coated.

Those comments are exactly what I need. They help me to make the story stronger.

So I spent a month on the second draft. That resulted in pages of comments that dealt with story problems, page by page.

After the third draft, came the line edits—dealing with the manuscript sentence by sentence, word by word, to ensure clarity.

Finally, at the fourth-draft stage, come the copyeditors, to bail me out. Not one, but several.

That's the pyramid: story as foundation, words in the middle and spelling, punctuation and grammar at the tip.

In my ideal educational world, stories would be graded this way: 70 percent on story, 20 percent on word choice, and 10 percent on appearance. And in my ideal world, students would choose one out of five stories to revise. The other four are just for fun, and the fifth is revised because someone else is going to read it.

CHAPTER 23

PYRAMID MIDDLE: WORD CHOICE

Nick Barrett is the main character of my novel, *Out of the Shadows*. Growing up in high-society Charleston, Nick did not know who his father was. There's a pivotal scene where someone calls him a bastard. It was the best word to use, not only because it was technically true, but the harshness suited the emotional content I wanted to convey for the scene.

But you won't find the word *bastard* anywhere in the book.

My editors and I spent a long time discussing whether to use it, and in the end, much as I didn't like their decision, they decided it was inappropriate for their audience.

I didn't resent cutting the word, however. I didn't like it, but I understood it.

Audience comes first.

Besides, they had already given me a lot of grace. It had been about three in the morning when I went through my final reading of the first draft, which was due five hours later. Bleary-eyed, I just began hitting *Accept* as spell-check suggested words.

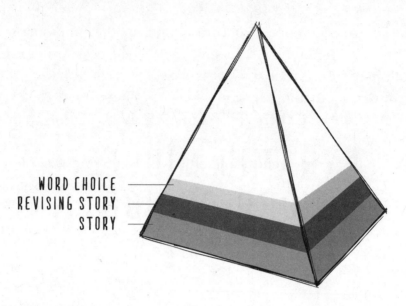

WORD CHOICE ——
REVISING STORY ——
STORY ——

A little backstory: In *Out of the Shadows* Nick Barrett's youthful marriage to a high-society girl is annulled almost immediately, and he has to flee the city or face prosecution for a drunk-driving charge.

Trouble was, my spell-check, for some reason, preferred *anus* to *anul*. So time and again, because of my haste to email the manuscript, my poor editors had some really big questions about my choice of vocabulary. When it came to the word *bastard*, I figured I owed them one.

I learned a lot from the line-edit process of *Out of the Shadows*. Every new novel I submitted to that publisher had at least twenty words or phrases I knew they'd insist on changing to make sure no one was offended. I did that on purpose, so that when I graciously agreed to those edits, my editors would not push so hard on the marginal stuff I wanted to keep.

I only ask one question when I'm helping students with their word choices: *Whose story is it?*

Unless the sentence structure is unclear or inappropriate, I see no point in telling a student what words to use or not use. Certainly not until that student is passionate about taking the craft of writing to another level.

Writers develop their own styles simply by writing. They need to be encouraged to find their own voices.

While I love most editorial advice, I resent being told how to write. At the word-choice stage, I most appreciate editorial advice that points out where the fabric of my writing is unclear or ambiguous. Or inappropriate for the audience. So when I ask whose story it is, the answer is simple.

It's the student's story.

Here's how I know.

In a church basement on the kind of crisp fall morning where orange leaves are a blazing backdrop, I saw how micro-management squashed creativity.

This was one of my first Young Writers' seminars for home-schooled children. Roughly thirty kids and about a dozen parents. I was at the front of the room, armed with a white-board, a blue marker and the stories I love to tell.

As everyone settled around the tables, parents sat beside their children. Half an hour into the seminar, it was time for the "four columns" exercise (which you can find online at rockandroll-literacy.com).

A nine-year-old girl started to write, with her father leaning over her.

He immediately corrected her and gave her a suggestion, which she dutifully copied onto the paper.

You can see where this is going, can't you?

Twenty minutes later, the story was finished.

She wasn't happy with it, but he was. Of course he was. It was his story.

We had a stand-and-stretch break, and then I informed the group that we had reached the scheduled time in the seminar when parents sat in the back and the kids worked alone. It was the only way I could think of to separate the parents from the kids.

It gave me a lot of satisfaction to watch that girl later in the day, as she wrote her own story, choosing her own words. It wasn't perfect like the one her father had dictated to her, but she was happy with it.

Ever since that morning, I make sure to invite parents to sit in the back of the room before we get started.

CHAPTER 24
PYRAMID MIDDLE: ADJECTIVES AND ADVERBS

Adjectives are good. I like adjectives.

"Hi. I have a cat."

"Really? What kind of cat?"

"A fat, stinky orange cat."

When I talk to kids about adjectives, these three lines of dialogue are all that it takes for kids to understand. They like how adjectives deliver a punch, and they have many favorite adjectives, most of them related to body functions.

Adjectives, good. Adverbs, not so good.

It's fun watching the reactions of the homeschool parents when I tell this to their kids during a seminar. Their eyebrows turn down and in, their lips tighten. I expect this reaction, which, of course, is what makes it fun to be blunt. I expect this reaction, because homeschool parents are teaching the way they were taught. Often, they've done a dozen lessons on teaching their kids to use adverbs.

I'd like to see a curriculum where teachers spend just a single lesson on adverbs, running less than one minute.

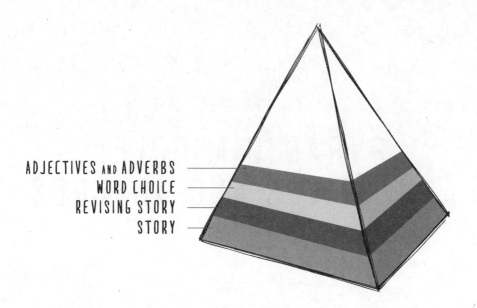

ADJECTIVES ᴀɴᴅ ADVERBS
WORD CHOICE
REVISING STORY
STORY

It would go something like this: "Boys and girls. Adverbs. Adverbs are words that describe action words like *run* and *hit*. Listen to this sentence: The boy ran quickly. *Ran* is the action word. *Quickly* is the adverb because it tells us how the boy ran. In this sentence, an adjective or two would be good so we could picture what the boy looked like. For example, the skinny, stinky boy with a booger half out of his nose ran quickly from the outhouse. Thank you. I knew you would like that sentence. Boys and girls, there are two more things you need to know about adverbs. One, adverbs often end with -*ly*. **Two, now that you know what an adverb is, use them only when you have no other choice.**"

Yes, I'd like to see a curriculum that exchanges time wasted on adverbs for lots of time on learning how to use verbs that are so powerful, they don't need help from adverbs.

Instead of *the boy ran quickly*, why not *the boy dashed* or *the boy motored?*

Instead of *hit the ball softly*, why not *tap the ball* or, better yet, *feather the ball*?

To get kids excited about verbs, I ask them to be sports announcers, finding ways describe how a ball or puck is hit. These are some of the words I hear:

Pounded.

Slammed.

Lasered.

Smashed.

Pulverized.

Come on. Isn't *pulverize* a great word?

There are three reasons I'd like to see most adverbs pulverized in teaching situations:

1. Promoting the use of adverbs also promotes the use of weak, imprecise verbs.
2. Promoting the use of adverbs when a strong verb is in place encourages a different sort of weakness in writing—redundancies, as in *dashed quickly*. (See Chapter 25.)
3. Promoting the use of adverbs also promotes inefficient writing. A strong verb is one word, while a weak verb and an adverb needed to prop the weak verb doubles the word count.

Kids love it when I slam adverbs. Maybe instinctively they know there is a bloated pomposity to adverbs, and who doesn't love bursting a bubble of bloated pomposity? Or maybe they are just tired of the emphasis on grammar and want to have fun writing stories.

CHAPTER 25

PYRAMID MIDDLE: REDUNDANCY

Pity my poor wife. Every time we fuel our car at a certain filling station chain, I rant for the next five minutes of our drive. Because of the sign posted at the pump.

Pre-pay before fueling.

Any guesses as to why I rant? It's the same thing I rant about when I hear these phrases:

PIN Number

Invest in the future

Traffic headed eastbound

My own personal opinion

I've got a very long list, as my golfing buddies know. When one of them declares, "I'll hit a provisional ball just in case my first shot is lost," they are now saying it to provoke me. That's because one day I made the mistake of pointing out that this common golf phrase is inefficient. "Provisional" means "just in case."

This is what Cindy hears after we leave that filling station:

"DOESN'T *PRE-* MEAN THE SAME AS *BEFORE?* HOW ABOUT THEM PUTTING UP A SIGN THAT SIMPLY SAYS *PAY BEFORE FUELING?* AM I SO STUPID THAT ONCE YOU'VE TOLD ME TO PRE-PAY THAT YOU NEED TO REMIND ME AGAIN TO PAY BEFORE I FUEL? AND HOW CAN SOMETHING THIS PATENTLY MORONIC HAVE MADE IT PAST ALL THE HIGHLY PAID MARKETING PEOPLE? EVERY TIME I PUT FUEL IN THE CAR, I NEED TO BE INSULTED? AND YES, I KNOW I'M SHOUTING."

Just like I shout at the radio when I hear a traffic reporter refer to traffic headed eastbound. "IN MY DICTIONARY, *HEADED* AND *BOUND* MEAN THE SAME HERE. AM I SO STUPID THAT ONCE YOU REFER TO TRAFFIC HEADED EAST YOU MUST ALSO INFORM ME THAT IT'S EASTBOUND? AND YES, I KNOW I'M SHOUTING."

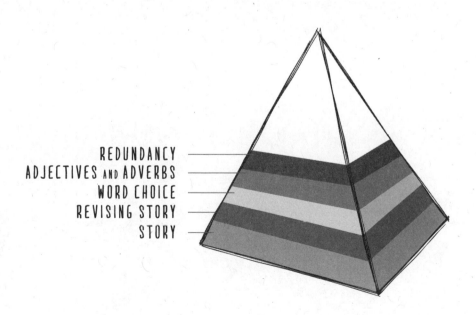

REDUNDANCY

ADJECTIVES AND ADVERBS

WORD CHOICE

REVISING STORY

STORY

Personal identification number number? Please make this stop!

Invest in the future? Doesn't *invest* imply *future*? When has anyone ever invested in the past!!

Give me spelling mistakes any day over redundancies. If you can tell a thousand-word story in seven hundred and fifty words, do it. Don't waste my time using words we don't need. Don't insult my intelligence by explaining it again with a different word. And trust me, I'm mortified whenever I get caught in a redundancy.

But that's just my own personal opinion.

CHAPTER 26

PYRAMID MIDDLE: FIVE SENSES

We are such visual creatures that we tend to write that way. I'm extremely guilty of this.

I refuse to worry about it during the first draft. Sure, if there's a sound or taste or smell or feeling that occurs to me, I'll put it in. But during the second draft, I'll go back with the goal of adding at least one of the other four senses to each page. It seems so arbitrary to me as I'm doing it, that I'm always afraid these "manual" additions will be too obvious to the reader.

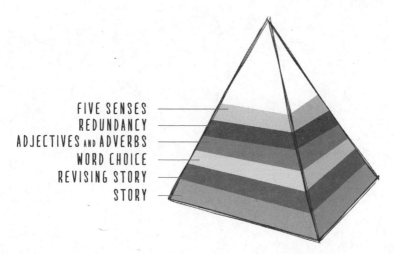

FIVE SENSES
REDUNDANCY
ADJECTIVES and ADVERBS
WORD CHOICE
REVISING STORY
STORY

When I get to the third draft, however, the additions don't seem artificial. Not only do they blend into the story, but I'm convinced they strengthen the fabric of the writing and make the events seem more real to readers.

CHAPTER 27
PYRAMID MIDDLE: WORD COUNT

I understand the traditional necessity of giving students a minimum word count. Otherwise reports and stories will be handed in at minimal length.

My response is, why not allow or even encourage minimal length?

Bloated writing is horrible writing. Kids who are straining to get their word count high enough put down sentences like this:

Although yet it was very and totally unnecessary for the tall skinny old and elderly man to walk down the wide broad street in the very wet rain, he slowly and deliberately managed to do this, making sure that he had a black wide umbrella above him the entire whole time so that not a single drop of water landed on his oily greasy short grey hair.

Why not impose a different goal: In report-writing, convince the reader of the point you are trying to make and make it a challenge for the author to do it in five hundred words or less. Four hundred or less. And so on.

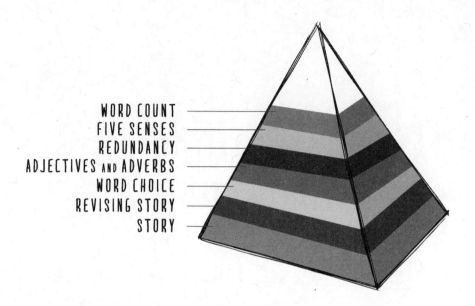

WORD COUNT
FIVE SENSES
REDUNDANCY
ADJECTIVES AND ADVERBS
WORD CHOICE
REVISING STORY
STORY

If a kid can do that in a hundred words, it will be a phenomenal piece of writing. In the previous chapter, I reminded you that we need to use all five senses in our writing. Hopefully you appreciated the brevity. But really, what more was there to say?

If your students are writing fiction, ask them to show you a problem, make it worse and solve it. In however many words they need.

I have a simple response to stories that are really short: *Wow, this made me giggle. Thanks! That was so fun, I'd love to see another one like this.*

If your goal is to get a student to write a minimum of five hundred words, I'd rather see the kid hand in five stories of one hundred words each, than have both of you endure the unpleasantness of trying to stretch out a single story.

CHAPTER 28
PYRAMID TIP:
SPELLING

When I tell kids that misspelling a word is a sign of intelligence, it almost always results in applause.

Most of them, especially the reluctant writers, hate spelling. One of the reasons they become reluctant writers is that their spelling mistakes have been pointed out to them so often.

There is not much sense to how words are spelled.

To me, *tuff* should be spelled *tuff*. Yes, I know the dictionary has it as *tough*, but do we need the *o*? And shouldn't *gh* make the sound of someone clearing a lot of phlegm?

After all the effort of learning that *gh* makes the "fff" sound, just when I'm ready to spell *sight* so it sounds like "sift," now you teach me that, hang on, putting a *t* on the backside makes the *gh* silent?

Come on, be fair about this, will ya?

But at least promise me that the *s* makes the "sss" sound. Thanks. Now that I've finally learned to spell *tough* the dictionary way, I'll just follow the rules and put an *s* in front of *tough*. Sure feels good to spell stough correctly.

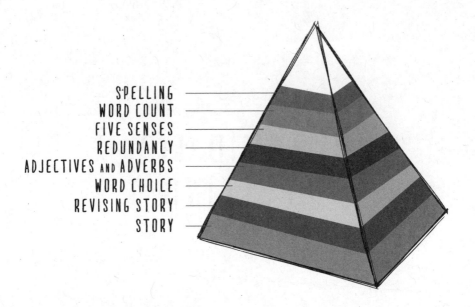

SPELLING
WORD COUNT
FIVE SENSES
REDUNDANCY
ADJECTIVES AND ADVERBS
WORD CHOICE
REVISING STORY
STORY

No wonder kids hate this stuff!

When I work with kids, I spend the first ten minutes saying how stupid, evil and moronic the dictionary is. Easy way to make friends. Easy way to make them feel better about misspelling words.

But then I abruptly point out that even though spelling sometimes seems senseless, it's still important.

The room goes silent.

So I write this on the board:

Deer sur, I wood like a jawb. Wood u higher me?

They always get the point.

If someone else is going to read your writing, I tell them, then you have to pay attention and spell words the way the dictionary spells them.

And, because my audience consists of kids, lots of them boys, I also tell them that spelling mistakes are like boogers.

No one is going to hear or remember anything you tell them if there's a big booger hanging from your nose. Too much of a distraction. Same thing with stories. Spelling mistakes become boogers all through your writing. Look for them and get rid of them.

I love hearing them announce they've just picked another booger. When, of course, they are referring to revisions.

Kids who are allowed to make spelling mistakes become better spellers; those who aren't often stick with their short list of safe words. My favorite story, written by an eight-year-old boy in one of my writing workshops, was about the octopus with eight testicles. Did I point out his mistake to him? Not a chance. His mother could deal with that.

CHAPTER 29

PYRAMID TIP: GRAMMAR

During writing workshops, I like to tell the kids about an afternoon at the zoo. I'd been walking with Cindy and the girls for a couple of hours. My socks had been driving me crazy. New pair. Too tight around my ankles. Souvenir shops at zoos do not sell socks. Taking the socks off would have resulted in blisters, so just past the tiger enclosure, I asked to borrow the nail scissors Cindy carries in her purse. I sat down on a bench, rolled up my right pant leg and snipped a vertical line from the top of the sock toward my ankle, cutting through the elastic. Instant relief.

As I began rolling up my other pant leg, Olivia, age eight, cried out, "Daddy, you can't do that!"

"Yes, I can," I said with satisfaction. I was irritated with the socks and revenge felt good.

"But you're wrecking your socks!"

My logic, I felt, was beyond reproach. No way was I ever going to wear those stupid socks again anyway. With my pants covering the socks, no one would notice the hatchet job.

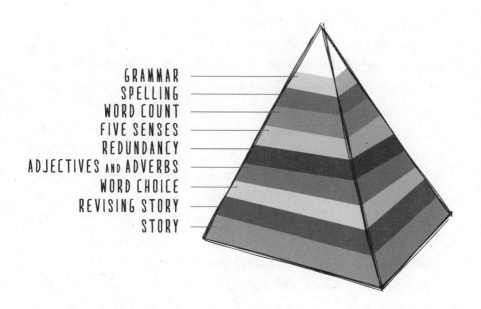

GRAMMAR
SPELLING
WORD COUNT
FIVE SENSES
REDUNDANCY
ADJECTIVES AND ADVERBS
WORD CHOICE
REVISING STORY
STORY

That wasn't the answer I gave her though.

"Olivia," I said. "I don't serve my socks. My socks serve me."

That led to exactly the question I'd hoped for. "What do you mean, Daddy?"

I did my best to explain, but in the end I'm not sure she was old enough to understand. Which was fine with me. I knew there would be plenty more opportunities, and I hope someday she will agree with me that people are more important than things.

You see, I know some people fret about scratches on their cars, about dandelions on their perfect front lawns, about whether the restaurant bill is split down to the last dime.

I don't want to waste that kind of emotional energy. I don't want to serve my car; I don't want to serve my lawn; I don't want to serve money. I'm selfish; I want all of those things to serve me.

When it comes to the writing pyramid, it's all about serving story.

So, with the writing pyramid on the whiteboard, immediately after telling the kids about the zoo, I draw a big looping arrow from *word choice* (in the center) to *story* (at the base).

Word choice, I argue, should serve story. Make a great story better by caring about words.

I draw another looping arrow from *spelling* (at the tip) to *story*. Spelling is there to serve story. Follow the rules of spelling, I tell them, because misspelled words distract the reader from story.

Another looping arrow from *punctuation* to *story*. Follow the rules of punctuation, I say, because it, too, will serve your story.

Just when I've got them lulled into thinking they know what I'm going to say about grammar, I draw one final even more looping arrow from *grammar* to *story* and tell them there are times when you need to go ahead and cut your socks.

Yeah. Grammar is there to serve story, but if breaking the rules of grammar makes the story better, do it.

Perhaps the most obvious place is dialogue. People don't use perfect grammar when they speak; if your characters do, they won't be believable.

Grammar also affects pacing:

My brother and I were walking along the creek in spring, just as the ice was getting soft. We saw a black kitten fall through the ice.

My brother took a step onto the ice. I grabbed my brother by the collar and pulled him back.

"That's too dangerous," I yelled.

"But the kitten will drown!"

It drifted slowly downstream, where the water was open. It meowed for help.

"Meet me at the bridge," I told my brother.

I got on my bike. Rode as fast as I could. Got home. Looked in the garage.

On the wall! A fishing net with a long handle!

Not long enough.

What else? What else?

There! The broom. Yes! The broom!

I threw some duct tape down the front of my shirt. Grabbed the net. Grabbed the broom.

I jumped on my bike. Rode one-handed as fast I could. Got to the bridge.

"Where's the kitten?" I yelled at my brother.

He pointed.

There it was. The kitten. Sinking lower and lower into the water as the current took it toward us.

I wrapped the broom handle to the fishing net, making it as long as I could.

Just in time, I reached down and plucked the kitten from the water.

I held the kitten to my neck. It licked my face and snuggled against me.

The grammar police, of course, would red-line my short story until it was a messy blur of ink. All those incomplete sentences. But those same incomplete sentences add to the urgency, which makes the story better. To me, that's enough justification for ignoring the grammar police.

Because no way am I going to suffer tight socks when I can borrow some scissors.

CHAPTER 30

PYRAMID TIP: PUNCTUATION

I put an oldie but goodie on the board: *"Let's eat Grampa!"*

After the giggling stops, I tell them that a simple mark will save Grampa's life.

"Let's eat, Grampa!"

They get that point too.

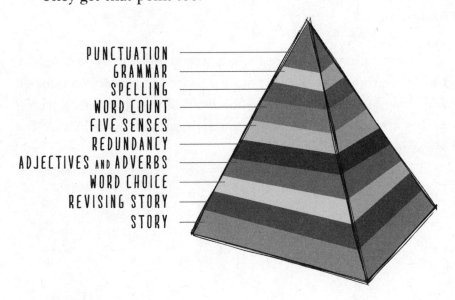

PUNCTUATION
GRAMMAR
SPELLING
WORD COUNT
FIVE SENSES
REDUNDANCY
ADJECTIVES AND ADVERBS
WORD CHOICE
REVISING STORY
STORY

CHAPTER 31

JOEY'S RUN AWAY HORSE

Frog Lake is a small town in Alberta, infamous in Canadian history as the place where the local Cree men began a rebellion against the white missionaries. (I know this because I have a friend whose great-grandfather, White Rabbit, burned down the church there, before joining Big Bear on a run from the authorities—a run that included taking hostages on a forced march. I also know something you won't find in the history books, because it had been passed down to my friend through her family. White Rabbit's words when asked why he'd burned down the church? "I hadn't seen a good fire in a long time." Someday, I want to write a novel about all of this.)

I'd been invited to the school at Frog Lake and was looking forward to the visit because of this personal connection.

What I didn't expect was to meet a Cree boy named Joey who would lead me to make a paradigm shift in the way I viewed kids and their writing.

At the school in Frog Lake, I'd been asked to help kids with editing. I sat in on a class and observed that Joey was, in the best sense of the word, a rascal. Nine years old, grinning each and every time he disrupted the teacher, who couldn't help but react with good-natured exasperation.

Finally, the teacher sent Joey into the hallway and closed the door.

From the other side of the door, Joey kept giggling and saying "hello," which led to laughter in the classroom. The teacher opened the door and warned of dire consequences if Joey made another sound. (This didn't reduce any of the wattage of Joey's amazing grin.)

The teacher closed the door again.

Seconds later, the giggling began again. Not from Joey, but from the kids in the class.

Joey had reached under the door and was wiggling the fingers of both hands inside the classroom.

The teacher opened the door and we all saw Joey on his belly, head arched high, grinning at the teacher. A likeable rascal.

Later, I had a chance to work with Joey on his story. Handwritten, in pencil, in block letters:

The Run Away Horse

Once upon a time there was a boy that loved horses. One day he went riding on his new horse. He named him Lightning. Sudenly Lightning started to run and Jason almost got bucked off so he brought Lightning home to the barn yard. Then he went for lunch and came back and Lightning was gone so he went to find him in the bushes be he couldn't find him. Three years later Jason was walking and saw Lightning and more horses. So he got Lightning and the other horses and lived hapily ever after.

I'd been looking for a piece of bad writing to use for an editing exercise, and this seemed perfect. I photocopied it, with permission from Joey and the teacher, not stating of course, that I wanted it as an example of "before" in a "before and after" piece for workshops elsewhere.

For the next few years, I blithely introduced *The Run Away Horse* to students and teachers and homeschool parents in various locations, asking them first to read the piece, pointing out that it was a great example of bad writing and then running through a checklist of editorial principles to apply to the writing.

Then came my revelation.

I was in Charlotte, North Carolina, at a homeschool convention, where I was speaking to roughly four hundred parents. All had received a package with the various exercises, including *The Run Away Horse.*

When I asked them to quickly read Joey's story, the auditorium became silent.

I had nothing to do during this silence, except mentally rehearse the points I was about to make on how to help a student edit, using Joey's story, of course, as the example.

Until this moment in Charlotte, I'd always presented this editing exercise to small groups of students or teachers. The silence had never been significant.

There is something intangible and significant, however, about the complete silence of a large group.

For a few minutes, each person in the auditorium was completely absorbed in *The Run Away Horse.* It struck me what an amazing and incredible feat Joey had accomplished, a feat that our children manage every time they put pen or pencil to paper.

At that moment in Charlotte, a Cree boy from Frog Lake, Alberta, was reaching across cultures and time and great distance to speak directly to men and women he did not know and would never meet.

Joey had accomplished this by scratching symbols on a piece of paper, using these symbols to tell a story that was important to him.

That humans can accomplish this incredibly complex task of using and interpreting symbols is a staggering intellectual accomplishment that we often fail to appreciate because it is so commonplace.

That humans are able to do this only a few years after learning to talk? Wow. Wow. Wow.

In the auditorium that day, after the collective rustling of paper that signaled that the parents had finished reading the piece, for the first time, I did not begin by stating that *The Run Away Horse* was a piece of bad writing.

Instead, I confessed the huge disservice I had done to Joey and his story, and how ashamed I felt. I asked them to celebrate with me that Joey had just reached into their lives, and to celebrate with their own children their amazing ability to do the same thing.

Sure, *The Run Away Horse* could be better with the help of an editorial checklist*. A piece of writing that can't be improved is very rare. But since that day, my first reaction to any piece of student writing is a sense of awe at what has been accomplished. I hope you agree that's a great place to start with any student.

*A checklist can be found at rockandroll-literacy.com.

SOME FINAL THOUGHTS

I prefer my focus to be on the end, not the means.

If incomplete sentences make the story better because it quickens the pace where I need to the pace to be quickened, the story must be served first by ignoring mechanics.

Where bad mechanics—spelling and punctuation mistakes, for example—distract the reader from a story, then story must be served by first focusing on mechanics.

Creativity is a beautiful mystery.

When your students put their imaginations on paper through words, let's glorify and praise this, first and foremost, and give mechanics no more or less regard than we would a pair of socks.

The book may look like it's over at the end of this page, but it's not. Because the dimensions of this book don't lend themselves to photocopy-ready sheets in an 8.5" x 11" format, the classroom story starters, along with instructions, can be found online at **rockandroll-literacy.com**.

I hope you will check out the website: you'll have access to story starters that work in homeschool and classroom situations for all writing levels.

Please feel free to share tips with other teachers in the forum there too.

Thanks for reading *Rock & Roll Literacy*, and I hope I'll have a chance to visit you and your students soon.

ACKNOWLEDGMENTS

Sarah Harvey, no one except you and me will know how much you helped shape and polish the ideas behind this manuscript. Thanks for everything, from beginning discussion to fifth draft! And thanks most of all for your encouragement through the process.

SIGMUND BROUWER is the author of many books for children and young adults. He loves to give his *Rock & Roll Literacy* presentation to kids (and adults) of all ages. To book a presentation, please contact Sigmund at rockandroll-literacy.com.

orca sports
High-interest | sports action

Titles by **Sigmund Brouwer**

- Mystery stories with sports themes for ages 10+
- Reading levels from grade 2.0 to 4.5
- Free individual teachers' guides online
- Accelerated Reader selections
- Paperback $9.95 each
- For more information visit **www.orcabook.com** or call toll-free **1-800-210-5277**

orca sports
Absolute Pressure
Sigmund Brouwer

9781554691302

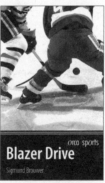

orca sports
Blazer Drive
Sigmund Brouwer

9781551437170

orca sports
All-Star Pride
Sigmund Brouwer

9781551436357

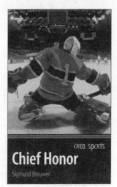

orca sports
Chief Honor
Sigmund Brouwer

9781551439150

Cobra Strike
Sigmund Brouwer

9781551437255

Oil King Courage
Sigmund Brouwer

9781554691975

Tiger Threat
Sigmund Brouwer

9781551436395

Hitmen Triumph
Sigmund Brouwer

9781551438733

Rebel Glory
Sigmund Brouwer

9781551436319

Titan Clash
Sigmund Brouwer

9781551437217

Hurricane Power
Sigmund Brouwer

9781551438658

Scarlet Thunder
Sigmund Brouwer

9781551439112

Winter Hawk Star
Sigmund Brouwer

9781551438696

Maverick Mania
Sigmund Brouwer

9781554690473

Thunderbird Spirit
Sigmund Brouwer

9781554690459